THE COLVER LECTURES IN BROWN UNIVERSITY 1965

ARZÁNS' HISTORY OF POTOSÍ

BARTOLOMÉ ARZÁNS DE ORSÚA Y VELA'S HISTORY OF POTOSÍ

By
LEWIS HANKE

Providence, Rhode Island
BROWN UNIVERSITY PRESS
1965

Copyright © 1965 by Brown University
All rights reserved
Library of Congress Catalog Number: 65-24779

Designed by Asher T. Applegate
Type set in Granjon by Connecticut Printers, Incorporated
Printed by Connecticut Printers, Incorporated
On Warren's Olde Style Wove
Bound by Russell-Rutter Company, Incorporated

To

GUNNAR MENDOZA

friend and colleague
whose scholarship and dedication
to the history of Bolivia
have helped to make possible
the Brown University Bicentennial
Edition of Arzáns'
Historia de la Villa Imperial de Potosí

CONTENTS

ILLUSTRATIONS

(Reproduced from the Brown University manuscript copy of Arzáns' History. Reduced 20 per cent)

INTRODUCTION

PLINY pointed out centuries ago that nature had evidently intended to make it difficult to locate precious metals, for they were usually found in nearly inaccessible spots. Potosí, the greatest single silver center in the Spanish Empire, admirably illustrates this supposition. *El Cerro,* or the Mountain, which contains the mines, was found by the Spaniards in the heart of South America at an altitude of almost 16,000 feet, higher than Mont Blanc, the tallest peak in the Alps. This Andean mountain stands in a dry and seemingly sterile land, with few trees or even shrubs for miles around, and the weather is often bitingly cold. The sixteenth-century Jesuit José de Acosta was greatly amused once in Potosí on recalling the dictum of Aristotle that lands became warmer the closer they were to the equator. No one opposed Aristotle's ideas lightly in those days, but Acosta's teeth were chattering despite Potosí's proximity to the equator.[1]

Visitors to Potosí today—few go there because of the cost, the inconvenience, and the cold—see there the great Mountain itself, and down below in the City impressive churches, the enormous Mint, and many other signs of departed glory. But they do not find there any general history of the mines and the City's dramatic life since mining operations began there in 1545. An Argentine historian lamented over a century ago: "Potosí, whose mines have enriched the world, has found no one who will publish her history."[2] At long last, a manuscript history of Potosí prepared by a citizen of Potosí, Bartolomé Arzáns de Orsúa y Vela, over two centuries ago has been published in its entirety.[3]

Colonel George Earl Church purchased a manuscript copy of Arzán's history probably about 1905 in Paris, and at Church's death in 1910 it was part of the library collection he willed to Brown University.[4] When the story of American enterprise in developing Latin America becomes fully known, the dreams and accomplishments of this engineer-entrepreneur will form an important chapter. His long life of work and travel in the vast region between Patagonia and Mexico, and his writings, helped to make known the geographical characteristics and economic potentialities of the area, particularly Bolivia and the Amazon Valley.

As I searched in 1932 and 1933 for material in Spanish repositories for a doctoral dissertation on the life and achievements of the Indian defender, Bartolomé de Las Casas, I first became aware of the "Imperial City of Potosí." The Spanish Republic had opened even the royal library in Madrid to historical investigation; I still remember the thrill of studying the extraordinary collection of manuscripts in the Biblioteca de Palacio. Professor France V. Scholes of the University of New Mexico and I systematically went through the collection and found there a two-volume manuscript history of Potosí. Though it was the depth of the Depression, though my principal concern was Las Casas, and though my wife, two small sons, and I were managing to exist in Spain on a fellowship designed to keep one thin graduate student alive, I then and there purchased a microfilm copy of the manuscript. On my return to this country I discovered that Brown University Library possessed the Church manuscript, which consisted of the First Part or some four-fifths of the whole work. Only the Madrid manuscript contains the Second Part, but it became evident that the manuscript of the First Part acquired by Church was decidedly superior to the corresponding manuscript in Madrid because it was more complete and more carefully prepared.[5]

Years passed. Then fate intervened, if that is the proper phrase. Dr. Lawrence C. Wroth, who has been my bibliographical mentor and historical counselor ever since my first visit to John Carter Brown Library almost thirty-five years ago, proposed to the Bicentennial Publication Committee that the Church manuscript be included in its plans, and Mr. David Jonah invited me to prepare the work for publication. By great good fortune, Dr. Gunnar Mendoza, the Director of the National Library and National Archives of Bolivia, agreed to accept joint responsibility for the task, and we have labored on it together in remarkable harmony.

No attempt will be made to describe in detail the contents of Arzáns' *Historia de la Villa Imperial de Potosí*,[6] but an English translation of its chapter headings is given here in the Appendix. The focus is on the life and work of Arzáns as a historian. I do not attempt to consider the literary aspects of the *History*, for this is a large and interesting subject in itself which is exhaustively treated by Dr. Gunnar Mendoza.[7] My object here is not to give a strictly chronological account of the silver mines and the turbulent society that grew up around them. We have not yet studied the voluminous manuscript records deeply enough to approach Potosí in that manner. My purpose is different and it is threefold: first, to place this particular history in the long, great Spanish tradition of writings on the New World; second, to establish the author as a man who exemplified a particular kind of American; and last, to indicate the riches his work contains for the study of a great city—one of the most important urban concentrations in the history of the Americas from the time when Christopher Columbus made known the existence of a new world until George Washington and Simón Bolívar insured its independence from the old.

Many individuals and institutions have helped the editors during the preparation of the edition of the complete text of Arzáns' manuscript history of Potosí from which this book stems.[8] In the completion of this book itself, originally delivered as the 1965 Charles K. Colver Lectures in Brown University, I have been aided by the discerning editorial eye of my wife, by a grant from the William A. Dunning Fund of Columbia University History Department, by Mr. Grant Dugdale, director of the Brown University Press, and by the careful revision of Mrs. Sandra Magrath, who expunged some of the inaccuracies and improved some of the syntax. To all of these I gratefully acknowledge my debt as well as to the prime movers, the Committee on the Colver Lectures and the Brown University Bicentennial Publication Committee.

LEWIS HANKE

Columbia University

ARZÁNS' HISTORY OF POTOSÍ

I

THE OTHER TREASURE FROM THE INDIES:
THE HISTORIES WRITTEN BY SPANIARDS
ON THEIR NEW WORLD

ASTONISHMENT and wonder were the immediate reactions to the New World of many Europeans from Columbus on. Hernando Cortez considered Mexico such a fair and favored land that he christened it "New Spain of the Ocean Sea." But perhaps his foot soldier Bernal Díaz del Castillo most strikingly expressed the sense of enchantment many conquistadores felt when he recorded in his *True History of the Conquest of New Spain* the dramatic moment in 1519 when the Spaniards, crossing the last mountain ridge, first laid eyes on the great Aztec capital Tenochtitlán lying in the valley below them, gleaming in its lake in the morning sun: "Gazing on such wonderful sights we did not know what to say or whether what appeared before us was real."[1]

Today, studying the copious records of the conquest of America, we may feel another astonishment that the companions and successors of Cortez were able to establish the rule of Spain so quickly in the enormous area of the New World. The English and Portuguese, for at least a hundred years after their first settlements, clung to the narrow coastal strips. Though the French roamed far and wide in Canada, they founded few towns of any size or importance. Spaniards, on the other hand, were not only in the forefront of the explosive geographical expansion following Columbus, when Europeans discovered "more territory in seventy-five years than in the previous thousand,"[2] but they also organized urban centers in many parts of their great domain. In less than a century after 1492 the ancient Spanish urban tradition had been so successfully implanted in America that there flourished the viceregal capitals of Mexico City and Lima, mining centers such as Guanajuato in Mexico and Potosí in upper Peru, Asunción in the middle of South America, Buenos Aires, Santiago de Chile, Quito, Bogotá, Caracas, Havana, Guatemala City and, far across the Pacific, Manila in the Philippine Islands. In Mexico alone in the fifty years after Cortez landed "a territory that could contain thirty or forty Iberian peninsulas had been claimed, and much of it settled, by a few thousand men."[3]

Another reason for our astonishment today is the attitude of the Spaniards toward the Indians. All European explorers and colonists encountered native peoples, but only the Spaniards met so many millions in the vast regions of their empire, which eventually reached from California to Patagonia. These, from the first landfall, they naturally called Indians—what else could they call the inhabitants of the lands they believed to be the Indies? The determination of the Spanish crown and the church to Christianize the Indians and the imperious need of Spaniards for labor to exploit the lands and mines for revenue for the crown and themselves resulted in a very remarkable complex of relations, laws, and institutions. The difficult, indeed impossible, double purpose of the crown both to Christianize the Indians and to obtain revenue inevitably led to a series of angry disputes, evil compromises, and some glorious episodes throughout more than three centuries of Spanish dominion. A few members of the Spanish nation dared to maintain that the purpose of the conquest was to benefit the Indians, not to enrich the Spaniards. These few insisted

3

that the only Christian way to achieve the high purpose of this conquest was by peaceful persuasion, not by force.

Today, in looking back on the total encounter of Spaniards and Indians, two developments in the experience of the Spanish conquerors hold special interest for us, living in a world whose tremendous multiplicity of cultures we know we must study and attempt to understand. First, never before in history had one people—the Spaniards—paid serious attention to the nature of the culture of the peoples they met; and, second, the controversies which developed in sixteenth-century Spain and America over the just method of treating the Indians led to a fundamental consideration of the nature of man himself.[4] As Francisco Romero, the Argentine philosopher, has expressed it, "There was developed during these years a new philosophy, a new vision of the cosmos, and a new science of nature."[5]

Historians who place great emphasis on the importance of prices have long emphasized the effect of the gold and silver from the New World on the fortunes of Spain in Europe. We know that only the timely arrival in late 1519 of Mexican gold from Cortez saved Charles V from bankruptcy at about the time his election as Holy Roman Emperor was announced in Barcelona. "It was the first real indication of the wealth of the Indies, a foretaste of the way in which the preponderance of the Hapsburgs in the Old World was to be supported by the resources they could draw from the New."[6] We also know that other loot from Montezuma's empire reached Brussels shortly afterward, where Albrecht Dürer, amazed when he saw it, marveled at the artistic ability of the Mexican Indians. Dürer wrote in his diary in 1520:

I saw the things brought to the King from the New Golden Land: a sun entirely of gold, a whole fathom broad; likewise, sundry curiosities from their weapons, armor, and missiles; very odd clothing, bedding, and all sorts of strange articles for human use, all of which is fairer to see than marvels. . . . I have never seen in all my days what so rejoiced my heart, as those things. For I saw among them amazing artistic objects, and I marvelled over the subtle ingenuity of the men in these distant lands.[7]

Another kind of treasure from the Indies is the extraordinary wealth of documentation which both excites historians today by its richness and depresses them by its quantity.[8] Friars and conquistadores wrote voluminous letters, many of which still remain in manuscript; the legalistic Spaniards produced an impressive quantity of judicial and notarial records in which are imbedded valuable historical data; and there are thousands of biographical statements drawn up by conquistadores seeking pensions or by others applying for jobs overseas. Even Cervantes requested a royal post in Peru, which he failed to obtain; the original petition is still preserved in the great Archive of the Indies in Seville. One wonders what changes the literary life of the New World would have seen if that immortal noble knight Don Quixote had experienced his famous adventures in America rather than on the plains of La Mancha in old Spain.

Fortunately for historians many Spaniards had a keen sense of history and a strong conviction that their actions would one day be carefully scrutinized by posterity. Columbus began the practice of writing about his experiences in the New World, and many others were moved to set down at least a part of its history, for the conquest so excited their imaginations that Spaniards came to look upon it as the greatest event since the birth of Christ. Even as the conquistadores roamed over vast areas of land and sea and missionaries attempted to Christianize millions of Indians, they collected historical materials and composed histories on a monumental scale.

In the days of Charles V the writing of history in and about America was often a sign of the Spaniard's conviction of his high destiny in the New World, his Renaissance zest for life. The everpresent ecclesiastics shared these feelings: scarcely a decade after the Franciscans first reached Mexico in 1524 they appointed one of their number to compose a history of their accomplishments to date and other orders did likewise. There was a spirit of derring-do, too, in many Spanish actions. The youthful conquistador Diego de Ordaz yearned to find out what lay beneath the outpouring smoke of a Mexican volcano and finally wrung reluctant approval from Cortez for his dangerous journey into the unknown only "in order that the Indians might see that nothing is impossible for a Spaniard." The Dominican friar Luis Cáncer set forth stubbornly to Christianize the Indians of Florida by peaceful means alone despite the prediction, later fulfilled, that he would be martyred. The mistress of Governor Pedro de Valdivia contributed to the defense of Santiago in Chile by personally cutting off the heads of half a dozen Indian chieftains held as hostages and rolling them down into the ranks of the invaders.

As the conquest proceeded, the crown stimulated, indeed expected, its subjects in the New World to report carefully and fully on overseas affairs and encouraged writers to prepare formal histories. On May 7, 1532, the Council of the Indies wrote to Emperor Charles V:

> Gonzalo Fernández de Oviedo, resident in Hispaniola, has had the care and inclination to write of affairs of the Indies; he offers to carry forward his work if he is given some salary toward the expense of collecting material and maintaining a clerk. It appears appropriate to be included in the Chronicle of Spain. He displays more ability than anyone over there. It would be well to order him to examine all those lands where he has not been and to send the reports to this Council in order that they may be edited and incorporated in the Chronicle of Spain and he should be given an annual subsidy.[9]

Charles V approved this proposal, and Oviedo began his great enterprise which twenty years later resulted in a large manuscript history, an encyclopedic work, prepared with the assistance of many officials. Since he did not relish the prospect of further travels in America—after all, he had already made the dangerous Atlantic crossing eleven times in an age when the voyage was often fatal—he persuaded the crown to order royal representatives in the Indies to supply the new chronicler with detailed reports of the geographical features, natural phenomena, and important events in their respective territories.

Oviedo has been termed a *pícaro,* an adventurer who made good, whose exploits helped Spanish writers to develop their famous picaresque literature. He was never satisfied; even after his final return to his homeland from Hispaniola, he complained to the future Philip II: "This cold air of Madrid where I was born is no longer suitable for a man who has been serving Their Majesties and Your Highness and your ancestors in the Indies for lo these thirty-five years." As a Paraguayan scholar, Natalicio González, has remarked, these are the "melancholy words of a conquered conqueror, who had imperceptibly become an American."[10] Here we see the first example of the influence of the New World on the lives and attitudes of historians who tried to tell its story, an influence which will be found strongly in the work of the Potosí historian, Bartolomé Arzáns de Orsúa y Vela, who wrote two centuries later.

Many other Spaniards, and some foreigners as well, prepared accounts of what they had seen or heard about in the Indies. The result was a considerable number of chronicles, in which fantasy at times mingled with facts. Even such a serious historian as Oviedo indulged in exaggerated accounts for the benefit of the folk at home. He wrote, for example, that he had heard of a Peruvian monkey that "was no less extraordinary than the griffins," for it had a long tail, with the upper half of its body covered with many-hued feathers and the lower half with smooth reddish fur. It could sing, "when it felt like it," in the same dulcet tones as a nightingale or a lark.[11] Oviedo also noticed that roosters crowed less often and less raucously than in Spain, and even the tomcats of the Caribbean made so little noise at night that his studies were not interrupted as they often had been when he was at the University of Salamanca. The chronicler of Peru, Pedro Cieza de León, who had been a famous conquistador at the age of twenty, heard in 1550 that bones of giants had been found there and thought that giants might still exist in that Andean land which was still only partially conquered and imperfectly known. Despite the many curious tales and imaginative conceptions found in these early chronicles, one gets the impression from reading them that Spaniards were deeply and seriously conscious of the historic importance of the mighty events in which they were participating and believed that there was indeed "nothing that a Spaniard could not do," or at least would not try to do.

The broad interests of these early chroniclers, which today would be dignified by some such resounding phrase as "interdisciplinary coordination," must be noted also. They viewed the conquest in the round and discoursed on disease and death, art and cooking, linguistic matters, child-raising, and a great variety of other subjects which interested them in the New World. Even the Dominican Bartolomé de Las Casas, best known for his staggering statistics of Indians killed during the conquest and for his polemical writings, also revealed a concern for education, a competence in psychology, and an interest in nature that even now are not fully appreciated.

As Spain developed a stable organization for governing the newly acquired territories, a demand arose for a truly comprehensive history of Spanish achievements and for adequate information to administer the far-flung empire. A decisive epoch for historiography began about 1570 when the president of the Council of the Indies in Spain, Juan de Ovando, decided that effective administration of the overseas territories required an archive containing organized information on previous laws and past events, adequate machinery for obtaining current reports, and an official historian. A detailed questionnaire was drawn up which required from every governor in America specific data on the history, people, products, climate, and geography of the territory he administered. Begun as a brief inquiry in 1569, this questionnaire soon grew to fifty items and eventually became a printed volume of three hundred and fifty separate questions. The "Relaciones Geográficas" that resulted from this scouring of the Indies for data remain an important but imperfectly known and used source.[12]

The first royal "cosmographer and chronicler" was appointed in 1573 to make use of the material collected by this method. Later he was given access to the documents sent to Spain as a result of the order of June 25, 1579, which instructed the principal royal representatives in America to search their archives for historical manuscripts and to dispatch the originals or authentic copies to the Council of the Indies in order that a true, general history of the Indies could be written. The royal chronicler was to devote himself to the task on a year-round basis, and it is clear from the description of his duties that the Council of the Indies was concerned both to record the deeds of Spaniards in the Indies and to learn in detail about their new lands. Spanish administrators showed their familiarity with human nature, or at least with the nature of historians who procrastinate or are perfectionists—it may be significant that Clio the Muse of history is never portrayed in the act of writing but always as poised to put pen to paper—for the Council of the Indies solemnly ordered that no "cosmographer and chronicler" should be paid the last third of his salary in any year until he had actually delivered some written history.

In most of the writings on Spain in America, Indians occupy an important place. The Aztecs, Mayas, Incas, and many others were not only exploited for their labor; they were also objects of an intense missionary campaign and their culture was studied. Though some of these studies were polemical in nature and sometimes produced tendentious results, the friars and laymen who sought to understand the life and language of the peoples they were conquering have been rightly termed the first anthropologists in the modern world, and the extensive reports they compiled remain valuable sources today. The names of Toribio de Motolinía, Diego de Landa, Alonso de Zorita, and especially of Bernardino de Sahagún will always occupy honorable places in Spanish American historiography because of their writings on Indian culture.

The most complete and objective study of Indian culture made by a Spaniard was the *General History of the Things of New Spain* by the Franciscan Sahagún, now being made available to English readers for the first time through the translation from the Aztec language being made by Anderson and Dibble.[13] Sahagún was an able and attractive friar—in his early years in Mexico his superior kept him out of the pulpit because some women in the congregation had their minds distracted from religious matters when he preached—who began to collect materials on the Aztecs in 1547. Ten years later his provincial ordered him to prepare a history of Indian culture. He devoted the years 1558–1560 to the systematic questioning of a dozen of the oldest and most knowledgeable Indians he could find, spending this period in the village of Tepepulco where he conferred with the wise men through young Indian interpreters who had learned Latin and Spanish. He used a carefully prepared list of culture elements as the basis for his investigation, and the Indians drew many pictures to explain their history. During 1560–1561 he moved to Santiago Tlatelolco and checked his data by using a fresh set of informants. Then for three years he examined and re-examined his material, revised the complete manuscript, organized the material into twelve books, each book into chapters, and each chapter into paragraphs. The result was a methodically arranged mass of carefully verified information on the gods worshipped by the Indians, their fiestas, their ideas on immortality and death ceremonies, astrology, witch doctors, rhetoric and philosophy, lords, governments, merchants and mechanical arts, vices and virtues, animals, birds, fish, herbs, trees, fruits, and flowers, and on the conquest of Mexico as the Indians saw it.

Sahagún completed this enormous task in 1569, half a century after Cortez invaded Mexico; the Indian life he described had already been somewhat modified by Spanish influence. The work remains, however, the most important and indispensable single source for the study of Aztec culture. His technical methods, his sympathetic and yet realistic scrutiny of a culture so alien to his own, and his determination to find out exactly what the Indians thought set his study apart from all the other anthropological writings of sixteenth-century Spaniards.

When comparative studies of the institutions and ideas developed by Europeans in the Americas are more fully elaborated—through the stimulus and activities of such institutions as the John Carter Brown Library—it will be established, I believe, that the broad-based anthropological investigations made by the Spaniards showed a valuable, even unique, approach to conquered peoples.[14] The great movement in history called the expansion of Europe constituted a remarkable attempt to bring to the so-called "underdeveloped" peoples of the world the ideas and techniques developed in Europe. The fact that we are still struggling ourselves to discover how to accomplish this objective without the element of physical conquest in a world of many races and many cultures gives the efforts of the Spanish anthropologists to learn the languages and understand the cultures of the Indians a familiar and poignant ring.

These anthropological studies were closely related to Spain's concern to work out a just Indian policy and to settle the question of the real nature of the Indians. The Spaniards were intensely preoccupied both with the just basis for governing their newly discovered overseas territory and with the nature of the Indians whom they were attempting to draw into the Christian world. Francisco de Vitoria, a Dominican professor at the University of Salamanca, discussed these matters with great vision and clarity in his lectures not long after the conquest of Mexico, and many of his students later went to America with their attitudes determined by his teachings. Vitoria remarked in one treatise, *Concerning the Indies:* "The Indians are stupid only because they are uneducated and, if they live like beasts, so for the same reason do many Spanish peasants." He also asserted that discovery alone gave Spaniards no more right to American territory than the Indians would have acquired had they "discovered" Spain. Vitoria and other Spanish political theorists of the time addressed themselves to the fundamental legal questions raised when Europe invaded America and, long before Grotius, laid down an enduring basis for international law.[15]

Most significant of all, the Spanish inquiry into the nature of the Indians and their capacity for entering into the Christian commonwealth led Spaniards to grapple with that ultimate problem—the nature of man himself. Of all the ideas churned up during the early tumultuous years of American history, none had more drastic implications than the attempts made to apply to the natives there the Aristotelian doctrine of natural slavery: that one part of mankind is set aside by nature to be slaves in the service of masters born for a life of virtue, free of manual labor. Learned authorities such as the Spanish scholar Juan Ginés de Sepúlveda not only sustained this view with great tenacity and erudition but also concluded, without having visited America or studied Indian culture, that the Indians were in fact such rude and brutal beings that war against them to make possible their forcible Christianization was not only expedient but lawful. Many ecclesiastics, especially Las Casas, opposed this idea scornfully with appeals to divine and natural law as well as to their own experience in America. The controversy became so heated and the emperor's conscience so troubled over the question of how to carry on the conquest of the Indies in a Christian way that Charles V at one point actually ordered the suspension of all expeditions to America while a junta of foremost theologians, jurists, and officials met in the royal capital of Valladolid to listen to the arguments of Las Casas and Sepúlveda. All this occurred in 1550, years after Cortez had conquered Mexico, Francisco Pizarro had shattered the Inca empire, and many other lesser-known captains had carried the Spanish banners to far corners of the New World.

The struggle for justice continued long after the great champions of the early days had gone, and generated historical literature of size and importance. For example, the town fathers of Mexico City and the energetic Viceroy Francisco de Toledo in Peru commissioned juridical treatises and histories with a definite political purpose—to prove that the previous Indian rule had been tyrannical and that Spanish domination in America was therefore eminently just; thus Spaniards could legitimately levy tribute upon the Indians and require them to work on the land or in the mines. Now began the preparation of a polemical literature which had as its principal objective the exaltation of Spanish contributions to the New World. This, in turn, called forth another polemical literature tending to prove exactly the opposite. These two viewpoints, usually characterized as the "Golden Legend" and the "Black Legend," still flourish wherever the action of Spain in America is studied.

The importance of the keen historical-mindedness of the Spaniards has not yet been fully recognized, for the enormous documentation available has been used only in part, and some of the most substantial works prepared during the more than three centuries of Spanish rule have been lost or printed only after long delay. An excellent and representative illustration of the other treasure from the Indies is the manuscript history in the Brown University Library written over two centuries ago by Bartolomé Arzáns de Orsúa y Vela and given the sonorous title: "History of the Imperial City of Potosí. The Incomparable Wealth of its Famous Mountain. The Greatness of its Generous Citizens. Its Civil Wars and other Memorable Events." In more than one million words it tells the dramatic story of the greatest and most famous single mining center in all Spanish America.

Except for the momentous discovery itself and the early conquests by Cortez and Pizarro, few themes have so continuously aroused the wonder and interest of successive generations as the fabulous history of the Potosí mines. Ever since the Spaniards first learned of the Mountain in 1545, Potosinos, and others, have composed poems, novels, plays, and histories relating to the tumultuous and romantic past of this Mountain of silver high in the Andes in one of the most desolate and inaccessible parts of South America. No one knows for certain how many writers have tried to tell its story, but one Bolivian has entitled an article "The Thousand and One Histories of the Imperial City of Potosí."

The early years of the Imperial City were given over to such frenzied exploitation of the easily available and rich silver deposits that history writing did not flourish. Not until the rule of Viceroy Francisco de Toledo (1569–1581) was life at the turbulent mining camp sufficiently stabilized for her inhabitants to be able to concern themselves with the past. When Toledo first visited Potosí in December, 1572, an Indian approached with a petition requesting that he be granted a pension as a son of the discoverer of the mine, which by then had become the dominant element in the economy of the viceroyalty. The methodical viceroy appointed Rodrigo de la Fuente to enquire into the matter and ascertain the facts. His report forms a part of the large and contradictory literature on how the Indians had stumbled onto the mine and then made known its existence to their conquerors. Toledo also stimulated the Florentine Nicolás del Benino, a member of the Medici family who had left his native city because of political difficulties, to compose in 1573 a valuable geological description of the Mountain.

Another veteran miner of Potosí, Diego Rodríguez de Figueroa, informed Viceroy Martín Enríquez in 1582 that he had been preparing "as a relaxation from his other activities" an account of Inca culture as well as a history of the first Spaniards in Peru including Potosí and had completed a painting showing all the mines and shafts in the Mountain to accompany his story. He had a definite objective, for he warned Toledo that unless the twelve Indians taken away from his mine were restored to his service he would be ruined. Many of the reports that today constitute a valuable part of the history of Potosí were designed to influence decisions at the viceregal capital in Lima or at the court in Spain, but rarely have they or the more formal histories been printed.

Among the Spaniards who drew up long reports for governmental authorities in the hope of influencing their action was an operator of a mill for reducing silver ore named Luis Capoche, who prepared a description of the discovery of the mine and its subsequent enormous development as well as an account of its general social and economic life up to 1585. The Capoche *General Account of the Imperial City of Potosí* provides an excellent picture of the first forty critical years of the mine.[16] Not a formal history developed on strictly chronological lines, or a tightly organized narrative, it proves particularly helpful on several fundamental aspects of Potosí during the early period 1545-1585: it gives a detailed inventory of the individual mine holdings and their owners, information on technological development, Indian life and labor, and the growth of the acquisitive spirit in that significant epoch of the expansion of capitalism in Europe—the sixteenth century.

Capoche's work was not published until 1959, but it was probably used in manuscript form in the early seventeenth century by Antonio de Herrera, the only royal "cosmographer and chronicler" who adequately performed his function of writing a general history of the Indies, although his account reached only to about 1556. An able and prolific official of the Council of the Indies, Antonio de León Pinelo, collected documents on Potosí, including the Capoche manuscript, in preparation for his never-completed history of the mines but died while waiting for more documents from the Indies; he suffered from the perfectionist spirit that afflicts some historians in all ages and all countries. He also suffered from neglect by the court in Madrid. For this hard-working and devoted royal servant, despite his long labors in the archives of the Council of the Indies which produced the material for the massive collection of the laws of the Indies, often cited by Spaniards to prove the magnanimity and Christian justice of their empire, was not appointed to the position he coveted as official historian of the Indies until shortly before his death. León Pinelo's grandparents had been burned as Jews in Lisbon, but it is likely that royal favoritism to others rather than religious grounds explain the court's indifference to his merits. In one of the manuscripts he left completed at his death, a genial work entitled *Paradise in the New World,* he located earthly Paradise in a precise spot in South America, which today is in the Mojos province of Bolivia. The four rivers mentioned in the Bible he identified as the La Plata, the Amazon, the Magdalena, and the Orinoco, and he believed that Noah's ark had been constructed near Lima on the western flank of the Andes. He clearly had become infected by what might be called "Potosí fever," for he showed the same tendency as other historians of Potosí to glorify and magnify everything connected with the mine. He, too, was fascinated by production figures and carefully calculated that the silver production up to the time he wrote "would be sufficient for a bridge or road of silver from Potosí to Madrid 2071 leagues long, four fingers thick, and fourteen *varas* wide."[17]

The citizens of Potosí were enormously proud of their City; a sample of this patriotic feeling is the "Información" Juan de Ayala y Figueroa presented to the royal tribunal in La Plata in 1609 and 1610. He recounted the great benefits the crown had received from Potosí silver and offered as evidence the testimony of some of the oldest and most respected inhabitants to support the demands of Potosí for lower-priced mercury and for reduction of the royal tax. One of his witnesses was eighty years old and had been in Potosí since 1545 when the mine was first exploited by Spaniards. The "Información" placed emphasis on the gifts of Potosinos to the crown, on their building of the large lakes to impound water, and their many other contributions to the improvement of the Imperial City. Potosí wanted the king to recognize its impressive additions to the royal treasury and to show gratitude by substantial concessions.

Repeatedly such documents, full of historical material not yet used, were drawn up in Potosí for presentation to authorities in La Plata, Lima, or Madrid; the representatives of the Imperial City

Page of the Brown University Library manuscript copy of Arzáns' History, *with stylized representation of the Mountain often placed at the end of a chapter. Several designs of the Mountain were used to give variety.*

que deves, y remedia tu neceſsidad; como
ya eſe Moreno que eſta contigo, eſtà libre
della. Deſpertò el pobre de Thomas a tiēpo
que el moreno Antonio ſe llegaba a el, à deſ
pertarlo para comunicarle ſu ſueño; y viſto
por entramboz la concordancia, creyeron
que Dios queria fauorezerlos a los dos; y aſsi
eſperaron el dia que no tardò en llegar el Al
ua. Al punto el eſclauo embiò à llamar a
ſu Señor, y venido, le diò quenta de ſu ſueño
moſtrandole como milagroſamente eſtaba ſa
no de ſus heridas, por donde ſe hazia creible
quanto le dezia. Thomas de Avendaño tam
bien refiriò el ſuyo; y aunque dudoſo to da
via el Veintiquatro D. Manuel, le dixo a
Thomas: Si fuere cierto el que las joyas eſtà
empeñadas en la tienda que dize eſte mi eſ
clauo os prometo amigo, de ſer vueſtro fia
dor haſta que vais, y ſaqueis el metal que de-
zis, y pagueis la deuda. Con eſto el Veinti
quatro fue a la tienda ſeñalada; hallò las
joyas, y muy alegre boluiò a la carcel, ſa cò
ſu eſclauo, y en adelante hizo mucha eſtima
cion dèl, como de quien era fauorezido de la
Madre de Dios. Luego fue a verſe con el Mer
cader acreedor de Thomas, y quedando a pa
gar por el ſaliò de la carcel eſte deudor: tra
bajò la mina, y conforme oyò la voz en tre
ſueños ſu cediò todo, pues brevemente ſacò
abundante, y muy rico metal: pagò a ſu a
creedor, y el quedò con buen caudal, moſtran
doſe ſiempre muy agradecido a la Madre
de Dios del Carmen. Tuuo noticias del ca
ſo el Illuſ.ſ. D. Don Chriſtoual de Caſtilla
y Zamora, Arçobiſpo de los Charcas en la
ocaſion; y como el bueno de Thomas de A
bendaño tenia en aquel miſmo tiempo a ſu
hijo mayor en el Colegio de S. Chriſto y al de
la Ciudad de la Plata, hizo grande eſtimaci
on del, aſsi por ſu virtud, como por la de ſu
Padre, y lo ordenò de Subdiacono, ſiempre
con la mira de acomodarlo en vn Beneficio:
aunque no llegò à eſte efecto, porque Dios ſe
lleuò a mexor vida à eſte Illuſtriſsimo Prin
cipe, y el ordenante ſe paſsò a la Ciudad del
Cuzco, adonde al preſente viue lleno de vir

El Illuſ.ſ.
D. D. Chriſ
toual de Caſ
tilla y Za
mora Arço
biſpo de la
Plata.

tudes, y letras.
Eſte miſmo año por el mes de Noui
embre, eſtando vn Indio llamado Anto
nio Ccolquema, hijo de Franciſco Ccol
quema, Sacriſtan de la Parroquia de S.
Martin, en el parage de Carachipampa
vna legua deſta Villa, recogiendo eſtiercol
de carneros de la tierra (que es lo que tan
to ſirbe para cocer a fuego aquel eſtimado
brebage deſtos naturales, que vnos llaman
Chicha, y otros Hathua) ſe armô vna te
rrible tempeſtad de granizo, y rayos. Viſto
eſto por el Indio Antonio, dexò de recoger
el eſtiercol, y apegoſe à vnos Eſpañoles que
venian a eſta Villa con ſus cargas, por bolverſe
con ellos. Apenas huuieron caminado ſolas
dos quadras quando cayò vn rayo, y al im
proviſo de ver el relampago inbocò el Indio
a la Madre de Dios de la Cādelaria de S. Mar
tin en ſu fauor. Pero entre muchos aſsi Eſpa
ñoles como Indios q̃ iban juntos ſolo diò el
rayo à Antonio ē la cabeça, de q̃ cayò en tierra
al parecer de todos muerto. Deſpues de recobrados
los q̃ con eſte Indio venian, ſe llegaron a el, y ſe le
bātando en braços, y a poco rato boluiò en ſi
diziēdo el Alabado, y luego ſe hincò de rodillas
y rezando vna Salve a la Madre de Dios, con
tiernas lagrimas en ſu lengua le comēçò a dar
muchas gracias por averlo librado de la mu
erte. Preguntaronle los Eſpañoles, como era
aquello, pues ſegun las ſeñales ſe dauan a en
tender que el rayo auia ētradole por el cele
bro y ſalido por vn oido? Aſsi es, dixo el Indio;
pero aveis de ſaber, q̃ yo ſoy muy devoto de la
Madre de Dios de la Candelaria de S. Martin
de cuya Igleſia es mi padre Sacriſtan, y entre
los dos tenemos diſpueſto hazer la fieſta en
dia del Novenario deſta Señora, que es de aqui
a quatro meſes, y porque mi muger vaya haz
endo Chicha, para juntar la plata q̃ ſe a de gaſ
tar en eſta fieſta vine à recoger hazia (que
aſsi llama eſte eſtiercol los Indios) y luego q̃
de el relāpago llamè à eſta Virgen Santiſsima;
diome el rayo, y quādo caì, la vide como eſtà ē
ſu Igleſia, y ella es quiē me ha librado: ayuda
me a darle gracias; y aſsi lo hizierō todos.

Por interce
ſsion de la
Madre de
Dios de la
Candelaria
de S. Mar
tin, libra
Dios a vn
Indio del
rigor del
rayo.

were famous for their pride and the persistence of their demands. But no history was authorized to bolster their case, despite the numbers of documents accumulating in royal archives: municipal records, judicial investigations, audiencia files, viceregal reports, annual statements on silver production, and much correspondence on religious matters. These documents, essential as they are for understanding the history of Potosí, were usually devoted to one single aspect of its life. No man with the historian's purpose as yet endeavored to tell the story of the mines as a whole.

When Bartolomé Arzáns de Orsúa y Vela began to write his history about 1705, he did so as a private citizen for his own pleasure, not as an official historian paid to keep his nose to the grindstone in order to receive a salary, and apparently without either financial aid or governmental recognition during the long thirty years he devoted to composing his work. He was simply a loyal Potosino who gloried in recounting the strange and marvelous events that had occurred in his birthplace. His was a labor of love, a tribute to Spain and to the New World. Though historical documentation continued to be collected as long as Spain held power, and writers in many parts of her vast empire produced historical works of many kinds until the revolutionary events of 1810 ushered in a new age, only the city of Potosí seems to have stirred one of its own citizens to prepare such a laborious, all-embracing history of its glories and its tragedies as the *History of the Imperial City of Potosí.*

Arzáns' decision to write the history of the Imperial City marks an important moment in the development of the writing of history in Spanish America. It was a new inclusive kind of history—not the story of a conquistador or an ecclesiastic, a royal official or a miner asking favors from the crown. Thus the spirit in which Arzáns recounted the history of the past century and a half was distinctive. He was a Spaniard born in the New World, called a *criollo,* or Creole, to distinguish him from the *chapetón,* or Spaniard newly arrived in America, and he told his story as one who had spent all his life in the isolated silver City. Arzáns' father and grandparents had come from Spain, and he was obviously glad to associate himself with Spain's achievements in the Indies. But he was also an American, critical of some Spanish actions and attitudes, and keenly aware that persons born in Peru were somewhat different from peninsular Spaniards. He exemplifies, therefore, what Jorge Basadre calls the "conciencia de sí," a New World feeling of independence and separateness growing throughout the Indies.[18]

This *americanismo* feeling had begun to be expressed in Peru at least a century before Arzáns began to write, as Aurelio Miró Quesada Sosa has shown.[19] It expressed itself in what might seem to be hyperbole, but it was, the Creoles were certain, the plain truth. As one Peruvian declared enthusiastically: "The poets have greatly exaggerated the wealth of Europe and the ancient East, but in Peru it is all true. . . . It seems incredible how many bars of silver have been extracted from Potosí alone."[20] Thus it is not surprising to find that the American-Spaniard Bartolomé Arzáns de Orsúa y Vela produced a special kind of history, as we shall see later from looking more closely at his life and his fascinating work.

If one were to believe what Arzáns said of his own deficiencies, one would scarcely begin to read his *History.* He admitted that his lack of learning and his innocence of Latin were responsible for what he termed his "rough style." He saw the task he had set himself as so difficult that one wonders at his temerity in undertaking it. But Potosí's fame and splendor gave him courage and he launched the work on a note of exaltation, for he rhapsodized: "The famous, always supreme, richest and inexhaustible Mountain of Potosí; a rare creation of the power of God, a miracle of nature, a perfect and permanent marvel of the world . . . an honor and glory of America."[21]

Arzáns had faith in the ability of those born in Potosí, was convinced that only those who witness events can adequately describe them, and was plainly writing to enlighten a European audience ignorant of America. He was close to the people, repeated many popular sayings, and in so doing revealed how Potosinos felt about themselves and about peninsular Spaniards, Indians, and the empire.[22]

Brushing aside his modesty, one finds the organization of the *History* impressive. His chapter headings are a detailed guide to the material in each chapter, and the year in which the events being treated occurred appears on every page of the manuscript, as if to underline the chronological nature of the work.[23] The sheer bulk of the manuscript is notable; it is doubtful that any other account of Potosí equals it in length. Arzáns' concern to provide so much information derived from his effort to tell the truth, which in his view the historian must always do, although he need not tell all of it. He realized that a native son of Potosí faced grave problems of objectivity, but he faced this challenge serenely. As a Creole he detested certain peninsular Spaniards for their supercilious ways and resented some royal laws. But he was a loyal subject of the crown, and his *History* helps us to judge how strong was the culture transplanted in the New World, even in far-off Potosí high in the Andes. To have produced one such historian may well be counted a considerable achievement by any empire.

Potosí has been famous for centuries for its silver production. But the *History of the Imperial City of Potosí* by that loyal and industrious Potosino Bartolomé Arzáns de Orsúa y Vela may some day establish another kind of fame for this great mining center. For this work is a prime example of that other treasure from the Indies which cannot be used in the countinghouse but which adds great riches to our knowledge of the history of Spain in America.

II

BARTOLOMÉ ARZÁNS DE ORSÚA Y VELA: THE HISTORIAN OF POTOSÍ

T HE HISTORY of the silver city of Potosí in colonial Peru, now part of Bolivia, might be reduced to a series of graphs recording the amount of silver produced each year, from the moment the Spaniards began to exploit the mines in 1545 until today, when the great Mountain yields tin instead of silver.[1] Such a statistical report would tell the economic story of Potosí, and some day when the archives have been more thoroughly searched, a chart of rising and falling production to indicate the curves of prosperity and decline in Potosí's history will surely be made. But that approach, so useful to economists and economic historians, would lack the human interest which principally concerns me, for a city's people and their lives are what give it meaning.

Potosí's great period lasted from about 1572, when Viceroy Francisco de Toledo insisted on the introduction of the use of mercury and stimulated the construction of impressive lakes which impounded water for power, until about 1650—a little over seventy-five years. By the middle of the seventeenth century the City had suffered three great crises so crippling that Arzáns at first planned to call his work "The Three Destructions of the Imperial City of Potosí." These events were the civil wars which raged between rival groups of silver-mad Potosinos in the period 1622–1625, the collapse of the great Caricari dam in 1626 which loosed a flood of devastating proportions, and the debasement of the coinage which very deeply affected the City about 1650. These three disasters successively weakened Potosí; after 1650 it lost its commanding position as the great silver center of Spanish America. The flush times, when its estimated population of 160,000 people surpassed all other New World cities and indeed most of Europe's urban centers, were over, and a steady decline set in. But just as Spain managed to present a powerful image of herself to the world long after her strength had waned, so did Potosí preserve her grandeur and her conviction of uniqueness long after her silver production and population began to diminish.

Our historian Bartolomé Arzáns de Orsúa y Vela was born in Potosí in 1676 at a time when production figures were plunging downward, and all during the thirty years he was composing the *History* from about 1705 until his death in 1736 Potosí's fortunes were steadily falling. What made him decide to become the historian of his City? Perhaps to the young man, surrounded by the splendid churches and fine houses of the glorious past and made aware of that past by the stories handed down from generation to generation, the City's very decay may have moved him to seek out the details of those years when it was the richest city in Spain's empire and the envy of all Europe. In one place where he is calling up the grand old times he says stoutly: "But how marvelous is Potosí even in her decline!"[2] And it is true that even after the glory had departed Potosí was still building. In the last years of his life the Church of San Lorenzo was under construction and was so impressive that one art historian of today calls it "the most famous of all the colonial works of art in Potosí."[3]

I shall not attempt to tell the story of Potosí chronologically but instead shall concentrate on the man who wrote so devotedly of his City and on what he tells us about the men and events that made the Imperial City a legendary silver center.

Arzáns filled some 1,500 large folio pages in close handwriting on the vicissitudes of Potosí, but he disclosed very little about himself.[4] Piecing together the scant information available from scattered sources, we learn that Bartolomé's father Mateo was born about 1635 in Seville during the long peregrination the historian's grandparents made from Bilbao in Spain to the New World, that Bartolomé was born in 1676 in Potosí, where he spent his life in modest circumstance until at the end of January, 1736, "fate cut the thread of his existence," to use the grandiloquent expression of his son Diego.[5] A psychologist would find little material with which to reconstruct and analyze him, for Arzáns recorded nothing about his mother, wrote little about his father except to characterize him as an "audacious Andalusian" who manifested on a certain occasion "arrogance and vanity," and noted of his son Diego only that he was skillful with the sword. The parish records in Potosí show that Arzáns was married on May 2, 1701, to a Juana de Reina, some fifteen years his senior. His references to her are limited to discreet generalities.

Except for some bits of miscellaneous information about himself in the manuscript, little is revealed of his family, his youth, intellectual formation, or other circumstances that would help us to understand the man who applied so much time and energy to the history of the Villa Imperial. He must have passed a quiet, relatively uneventful existence if the scarcity of documentation about him is a true indication. In a community much given to public and private disputes, no evidence of his involvement in the bitter litigation so characteristic of Spanish colonial life has yet come to light. Arzáns, despite his modest circumstances, never seems to have appealed to the town fathers or royal officials for assistance, nor even to have informed the local dignitaries of his great enterprise which surely would have appealed to their pride in Potosí. This silence must have meant that Arzáns did not wish the world generally to know of the task which was absorbing so many hours of his life. Perhaps he considered the composition of the *History* a deeply personal undertaking which he could do best in obscurity, since it dealt with controversial matters. Unless more documents on his life are discovered, we must conclude that Arzáns was largely a self-educated person with little formal schooling, who saturated his mind with a wide range of learning, old and new, and applied it to a large historical work while he lived thousands of miles away from the cultural centers of Europe and even at a considerable distance from the universities established by Spain in the New World.

Why was the *History* never published during the author's lifetime? Why was it allowed to remain in manuscript from Arzáns' death in 1736 until 1965 when the Brown University Bicentennial Publication Committee resolved to bring out the first complete edition? Potosí was considered by many Spaniards "the principal power" in all the realm of Peru. Potosinos had long cherished a lively sense of their own importance, and the first coat of arms of the Villa Imperial, which Charles V bestowed upon the City, faithfully reflects this proud Texan-like spirit: "I am rich Potosí, the treasure of the world, the king of the mountains, and the envy of kings." When Arzáns was writing (1705–36), silver production of the mines had so declined that Potosí had lost its preeminence, but the pride of the Potosinos did not diminish nor did they abandon their passionate conviction that the Imperial City constituted a spectacular part of the history of America and indeed of the whole world. Moreover, the *History* contains so much gore and glory, so much sex and saintliness, so much detail on the almost incredible story of the Andean mining center, that its nonpublication for over two centuries after the manuscript was completed does in truth require explanation.

Arzáns apparently guarded his treasure well during the years he labored on it, for from the first he feared criticism and expected that some one would cast aspersions on his writings.[6] Historians in Spanish America early learned that theirs was a dangerous life. Augustín de Zárate arrived in Peru at the time of the civil wars there in the sixteenth century with the idea of preparing a history but soon discovered that this would be "most imprudent," since the conquistador Francisco de Carbajal, familiarly known as "the Demon of the Andes," had promised to kill anyone who dared to write of his swashbuckling actions. In the early seventeenth century even the official historian,

Antonio de Herrera, had to defend himself in Madrid in a lengthy lawsuit against the angry Count of Puñonrostro, who charged that Herrera had maligned his ancestor, the notoriously cruel conquistador Pedrarias. About the same time, the Dominican historian in Guatemala, Antonio de Remesal, had to go into hiding from Spaniards there who were enraged by his description of the conquistadores in his history of Chiapa and Guatemala. So it is not surprising that Arzáns at times omitted the names of evildoers in his text. He did not withhold criticism when he considered it well founded, but he seemed conscious of readers looking over his shoulder ready to censor his work or to attack him.

Despite Arzáns' secretive attitude, the *History* became known to a few persons in the Villa Imperial shortly after he began to write in 1705. He evidently allowed some favored ecclesiastics to see his manuscript and even to use in their sermons the harrowing tales and edifying incidents recorded in the *History* as they strove to impress upon the licentious and quarrelsome Potosinos the need for Christian charity and Christian morality. Later, the Dominican Josef Lagos preached nine successive nights using examples from the *History* on the epidemic of 1719, a terrible experience during which Arzáns had cared for the sick and had helped to bury some of the 20,000 dead.[7]

Others who somehow learned of the preparation of the manuscript feared that it might include unpleasant reports of them or their friends, and once an indignant citizen threatened to kill the historian for writing about the misdeeds of his relative, "a certain judge." Arzáns saved himself only by going into hiding for a time. On another occasion a royal officer threatened to destroy both the historian and his writings, for Arzáns had included accounts of the evil administrative practices of that individual, one of Arzáns' favorite themes being official corruption. Fortunately for us all, Arzáns in particular, the officer died before he could put his threat into effect.

These and similar incidents led the historian to keep the contents of his manuscript as secret as possible and, to throw evilwishers off the scent, he occasionally leaked the false news that it had been dispatched to Europe for publication. These stratagems were not wholly successful, and Arzáns was approached by various persons who offered large sums for the manuscript so that it could be printed, but no such offer was accepted despite the writer's financial needs. Even the French sea captain who offered a considerable payment for the privilege of taking the manuscript to Paris as a gift to his monarch was refused, for the loyal Potosino felt that it would be improper for anyone except his own king in Spain to receive his work. Yet when Don Pedro Prieto Laso de la Vega offered to take the *History* to Madrid, Arzáns again refused, fearing that it might be lost en route, a calamity that had more than once occurred to the compositions of authors in the New World, and not only by reason of shipwreck. When Arzáns died in 1736 at the age of sixty, the lifework on which he had lavished thousands of hours and much creative energy was still unpublished.

His son Diego tried to continue the work for a year or so, although clearly not equal to it; he apparently had financial difficulties, and it seems he sold the copy of the manuscript in his possession not long after his father's death.[8] This copy contained both parts of the work and from the description given of it at this time appears to have been the Madrid manuscript.

The *History* was not forgotten, however, even though its location was apparently kept secret. When Diego died suddenly in 1755 a high official in Potosí, probably the corregidor, instituted immediate and searching inquiries concerning its whereabouts. At length it was discovered in the hands of an ecclesiastic who was determined to keep it. Official influence had its way, however, and by 1756 the manuscript was on its way to Madrid, where eventually it came to rest in the king's private library. But it was never published, and today's visitors to the handsome Biblioteca de Palacio can still see it in just about the same condition as it was when the triumphant corregidor in Potosí dispatched it to Madrid over two hundred years ago. The origin and movements of the manuscript of the First Part used for the basis of the Brown University Bicentennial Edition, which Colonel George Church acquired while living in London, have not yet been ascertained.

While mystery has characterized the odyssey of the manuscripts of the *History*, the history of various attempts to publish it has been a lamentable one.[9] What little is known on these interesting

Title page of the Brown University Library manuscript copy of Arzáns' History. *Above on the left is the coat of arms bestowed on the Imperial City by Emperor Charles V, with the inscription: "I am rich Potosí, the treasure of the world, the king of the mountains, and the envy of kings." The imperial crown surmounts the Mountain, on a white field, and at the side are the "Plus Ultra" columns of the Emperor. Philip II gave the second coat of arms (upper right) on August 10, 1565, which includes the imperial eagle on which is superimposed two castles and two lions, the imperial crown as the crest, and as an ornamental border the Golden Fleece.*

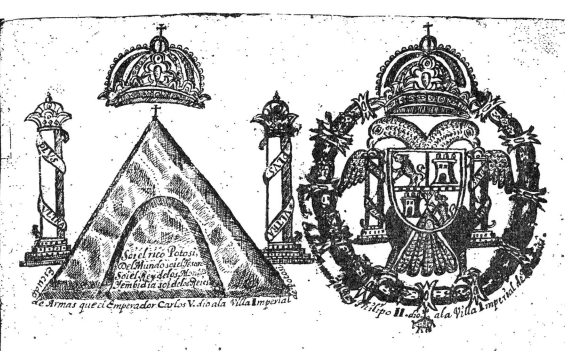

de Armas que el Emperador Carlos V. dio a la Villa Imperial   Philipo II. dio a la Villa Imperial de ...

HISTORIA
DE LA
VILLA IMPERIAL DE POTOSI
RIQVESAS INCOMPARABLES
DE SV FAMOSO CERO
GRANDESAS DE SV MAGNANIMA POBLACION
SVS GVERAS CIVILES
Y CASOS MEMORABLES.

Por D. Bartholome Arzáns de Orsúa y Vela, natural
de dicha Villa.

Dirigida

DE D. Luis Josef de Lacòa,

matters has been brought together in the printed edition, and we can now turn from the author to the *History* itself to see how this treasure house of information and fantasy on the history of the Villa Imperial de Potosí was built and with what materials.

Bartolomé Arzáns de Orsúa y Vela does not state exactly when he first began his historical labors.[10] By 1702, shortly after his marriage, he had apparently gathered many manuscripts and other materials, had sketched out an outline of a projected history in the form of a chronologically organized manuscript list of important events, and had optimistically planned a larger and more general history.

Arzáns started the first chapter of his larger work in 1705 and for the next few years wrote so rapidly that by 1708 he had completed the story of 140 years of the total time span of 190 years of the *History,* which covers the period 1545 to 1736. During this period of feverish composition he also made considerable progress on another compendious work, the "New and General Province of Peru," which must have involved much research. He explained that this second historical composition was intended to provide detailed information on "the monstrous wealth Potosí yielded in slightly less than ten years . . . how, when, and by whom each one of the mines was found, . . . the intolerable labors suffered by the men who discovered the mines and acquired the gold and silver in harsh and sterile lands lacking everything necessary for human life." By 1721 this work was practically completed, but Arzáns was a perfectionist in spirit and decided he needed one more document. Meanwhile, in order to satisfy the wishes of four eminent persons in Lima, he included a portion of the manuscript in the first chapter of the Second Part.[11] The sample that he gives does not whet the reader's appetite for more, since it is a mass of statistics and geographical names. His description of it indicates that much labor must have gone into its composition, but unfortunately this manuscript has apparently been lost.

Perhaps the simultaneous labor on two historical works was too much for his health, for he seems to have slowed down. He prepared the text of the *History* covering the years 1708–1720 in a much more leisurely fashion, and during the final fifteen years until his death in 1736 apparently wrote up the events of each year as they occurred in reportorial fashion.

Why this extreme change in pace after 1708? Perhaps his spirit weakened. He may have exhausted the materials he had brought together or was perhaps weary of his confining task. He may even have been somewhat like Penelope and never really wanted to end the work. His unpleasant experiences with angry Potosinos who did not like what they suspected (or knew) he wrote about them or their ancestors may have convinced him that discretion was the the better part of valor. Or had the adding of new material year after year come to be the chief reason for his existence, so that he could not bear to bring his lifework to a close? There is a mystery here, for in 1708 at the beginning of Book X in the First Part Arzáns believed it would be his last book and expressed great eagerness to finish it. Yet the story went on and on. He embarked upon a Second Part which he never completed. Despite his remarks from time to time on the transitory nature of this life on earth, he seemed to have avoided making arrangements for either the completion or publication of the *History.*

Arzáns struck such a mournful note in 1721 on beginning the Second Part that it is surprising he was able to summon up the courage to continue to write for the remaining fifteen years of his life. He gave the impression that he felt the world was running down and that the final part of his history would record only dark and disagreeable hours in the life of his beloved Potosí, which was indeed declining in silver production. Whatever his reasons, Arzáns left the fruit of over thirty years of labor unfinished and unpublished at his death.

Diego, who had inherited his father's manuscripts and attempted to continue the *History,* managed to write eight chapters, but his narrative is little more than a collection of miscellaneous information and weird tales of giants, bisexual beings, two-headed cats, women who give birth to serpents, and other monstrosities. When the manuscript of the Second Part stops abruptly, in the middle of a sentence, the reader feels relief rather than disappointment.

Did Diego become discouraged at the heavy task of continuing his father's massive work in the face of intimidation by those citizens of Potosí whose misdeeds were being chronicled? Did he lack that dedicated, almost fanatical, spirit required for the successful completion of any large enterprise? It was, after all, not his own conception, and he probably had little time or energy left over for historical composition after earning his living. In any case, he disposed of his father's manuscript for a few pesos to a nameless ecclesiastic, who fortunately kept it intact until the official inquiry in 1756 set in motion the series of events which finally sent the *Historia de la Villa Imperial de Potosí* on its way to Spain.

Now that the text of the *History* has been printed, we can see what kind of narrative Arzáns worked on for so many years and what sources he used to document his story.[12] Following the hallowed tradition of historians, Arzáns has provided twentieth-century readers with a great deal of information on the materials he used. Over forty authors had already written on various aspects of the Villa Imperial, he explained, and he had consulted all of them, besides other "accounts, archives, and manuscripts" of interest. In addition, he quoted from a vast array of printed books on the Indies, which range from the 1553 *Crónica del Perú* by the youthful conquistador Pedro Cieza de León down to publications that appeared as he was writing in the first third of the eighteenth century. He must have had either a considerable personal library or access to ecclesiastical and private collections in Potosí. Some of the more enlightened citizens of the town probably did read widely despite various restrictive laws intended to control the importation of undesirable ideas. Though sometimes it seems that Arzáns must have endeavored to arouse his reader's admiration by the very multiplicity of references to learning old and new, sacred and profane, no one can dip even casually into the *History* without concluding that its author had used a large reservoir of information from many sources. He did not limit himself to documents, printed or in manuscript; he also wove into his chapters many of his own personal experiences as well as many examples of oral tradition, which has long been a characteristic element in the annals of Potosí.

Among the richest sources for the *History* were the works of certain historians whom Arzáns quoted and referred to on many of his pages, although we must take his word for their existence since we cannot find their works. Captain Pedro Méndez was the first of these historians to reach the Villa Imperial.[13] Arzáns says he was a grandson of that attractive Renaissance figure Diego Méndez, a follower of Erasmus and companion of Columbus. Captain Méndez was born on the island of Hispaniola in the Caribbean but did not remain there long, moving frequently from one place to another around the empire, as Spaniards and their descendants did in the early explosive days of the conquest. We are told that Pedro Méndez was in Mexico City when he saw a document about Potosí that whetted his curiosity, for it included a sketch of the Villa Imperial and told of the square-shaped cloud that was supposed to hover directly about the great Mountain near the town in which the mines were to be found. When the cloud moved away from the Mountain, it was said, silver production fell calamitously, to the rage and despair of the Potosinos. Méndez was skeptical of this phenomenon and left Mexico for Potosí, while still quite young, principally to see the cloud. On arrival he could not find it, but he stayed on for some sixty-six years and, when he died in 1631 at the ripe old age of eighty-six, was a highly respected citizen and chronicler. This is not so surprising as it may seem, for despite the rigors of the Andean location of the mines, some Potosinos enjoyed lengthy life spans. Luis Capoche in his *General Account* of 1585 mentions a miner 120 years of age who climbed to the top of the Mountain of silver "from time to time when he felt like it." Arzáns' wife died at over eighty years of age, and the legal records of Potosí contain a number of references to citizens who had long resisted the cold, the altitude, and the harsh living conditions which characterized the Villa Imperial.

Captain Méndez, a gallant and attractive gentleman who fought in a number of battles against the Indians, also composed a history of Potosí which covered the years 1545–1626. Unfortunately he incurred the enmity of several persons, including another historian, who persuaded the viceroy to have him arrested in 1627 and taken to the capital Lima for trial. He was acquitted but not allowed to return to Potosí, and he died four years later without publishing his manuscript.

Arzáns held Méndez and his history in high esteem. He called him a "great investigator of the glories of Potosí," frequently quoted his work, and testified that he had been able to corroborate Méndez's statements by his own researches in archives and libraries. Méndez was notable for including in his work data on prices of daggers, hats, and clothes as well as jokes and literary maxims. All the City regretted that the "Historia de Potosí" of the brave and popular Captain Méndez was never published, said Arzáns, who narrated with satisfaction the unpleasant and untimely deaths of all the enemies of Méndez who had been responsible for his imprisonment.

Yet Captain Méndez and his work are known to history only through the pages of Arzáns' History, and lacking any other proof of his existence one may ask whether Arzáns himself created Captain Méndez to add to his galaxy of chroniclers. Can his imagination have been fertile enough even to compose a series of histories and to provide their reputed authors with exciting biographies as well? If this is so, Arzáns performed deeds of daring probably unique in the literary history of Spanish America. But we shall probably never know.

The author most frequently quoted by Arzáns is Don Antonio de Acosta, whom he designates as "a noble Portuguese who wrote in his own language."[14] And, in fact, Portuguese miners, merchants, ecclesiastics, and others were to be found in Potosí, as in many other parts of the Spanish empire from the earliest days. They not only engaged profitably in many enterprises there but also wrote careful descriptions of what they saw in the New World. Arzáns often referred to Acosta as an eyewitness of the many events he described, from the time he arrived in Potosí about 1579 until his death in 1657 at almost one hundred years of age.

Acosta wove many different kinds of material into his story. He speculated on how Potosí received its name, remarked upon the large fortunes gained by tavern keepers, gave details on the discovery of certain large precious stones, and described so vividly the terrible hurricanes that occasionally afflicted the town that one can fairly hear the wind whistle as it sweeps through the narrow and crooked streets and see the market goods set out in the plaza by Indian women swirled away in the air by the violence of the wind. Acosta recorded the uncovering during the excavations for the Dominican church of a strange skeleton which had teeth as large as dove's eggs and calculated that so much silver had been extracted from the mines that it would rise to the same height as the Mountain if all piled up together. He gave meticulous and exuberant detail on the numerous and costly fiestas that Potosinos organized at every possible opportunity, and Arzáns often referred the reader to him for more information, as though Acosta's history were available at that time.

Because Acosta's experience went so far back into the early years of Potosí, his description of the first frenetic days of the mining center is especially valuable. The Spaniards hurriedly built temporary houses, no one bothered to establish streets, and in eighteen months 14,000 persons had arrived to begin what one might call The Great Silver Rush of Peru. Acosta subscribed to the same theory as Arzáns that a history should be full of spicy stories. Among others, he related how the Andalusian Gaspar Martínez resisted the temptations of a lewd woman and became one of the most pious friars in the Villa Imperial, and how some Potosinos fought each other naked from the waist up on a bitter winter's day to demonstrate their valor and their contempt for normal precautions.

Acosta's piety and interest in the City's religious life were strong; he reflected well the spirit of his age which has been termed "a pious century." He gave numerous accounts of miracles, demons, catastrophes visited upon Potosí on account of the sins of its inhabitants, as well as examples of both great charity and the lack of it. Acosta personally knew one Potosino so holy that after his death he was venerated as a saint; twenty years after burial in 1625, Acosta assures us as an observer when the tomb was opened that his body "was whole, exhaling an admirable fragrance."[15]

Acosta naturally paid considerable attention to his fellow Portuguese and provided much information on their participation in the affairs of the Villa Imperial: how they fought in the bitter civil wars, how a Portuguese doctor practiced medicine there, how splendid a corregidor was General Pereyra and how rich was Antonio Alonso de la Rocha Meneses. It is easy to see that Acosta both maintained his pride as a Portuguese and was also a loyal son of Potosí who gloried in its grandeur.

But did this "noble portugués" actually live in Potosí and, if so, was he really the author of a history printed in Lisbon? No copy of Acosta's *Historia de Potosí* has yet been located, despite my own prolonged efforts and much skilled searching by scholarly friends in Portugal.[16] So complete is the silence on Acosta of the standard bibliographies that the question must be asked whether his detailed account of the Villa Imperial ever existed. His name does not appear on any list of foreigners in Potosí come to light thus far, and no one but Arzáns ever mentioned the work. Arzáns, however, cited him so confidently and so frequently that it seems likely that Acosta actually lived and prepared a volume which either was never printed or issued in such a limited edition that no copy has survived to the twentieth century. Lacking that single copy, in either manuscript or printed form, we have Arzáns' work as our only source of information on Acosta's very life and thus his history.

Bartolomé Arzáns de Orsúa y Vela loved literature and considered himself a man of letters. He showed an unusual affection for the poet Juan Sobrino whose history of Potosí in verse was left incomplete at the time of his death.[17] Arzáns cited the poem fairly frequently, always referred to it as an "obra elegante," and clearly had a soft spot in his heart for this poet who was apparently also a fighter in the terrible civil wars that erupted in Potosí in 1622. Contemporary documents have been discovered in a Bolivian archive on one "Lieutenant Juan Sobrino" who figured as one of the minor leaders in these wars and who in 1623 was charged with being one of the band that broke into the house of the corregidor, Felipe Manrique, killed half a dozen men and wounded others, and then set fire to the house of the king's appointee before escaping without injury.

Arzáns always took Sobrino seriously, quoted lines from his verses from time to time as though he had some favorite passages, and mentioned that the "historian-poet" also wrote a theatrical piece entitled "Prosperity and Decline of the Incas of Peru," which was acted in 1641 as a part of one of the innumerable fiestas the Potosinos indulged in with such delight. Sobrino's drama was one of four plays put on after three days of bullfighting, and Arzáns solemnly assured his readers that "it was worthy of being shown in the best theaters in the world."[18] The drama gave the detailed story of the rise and fall of the Inca empire; Arzáns remarked that not only the Spaniards followed the action of the play with great interest but that the Indians did also and uttered piercing cries as they witnessed the successive defeats of their ancestors. Since most of Potosí's Indians were drafted labor for the mines, one can imagine that those cries came from the heart.

Though it is uncertain that "Lieutenant Juan Sobrino" who fought in the civil wars was the poet who composed a history of Potosí in elegant octaves, poetry as well as fighting was certainly cultivated in those tumultuous years. According to Menéndez y Pelayo, the Spanish literary authority, the writer who "truly enriched the Mountain of Potosí with veins of poetry more precious than the silver in the mountains" was Luis de Ribera, who in 1612 completed there his volume, *Sacred Poems*.[19] Thus the poet Juan Sobrino, if in truth he lived in those turbulent years of the early decades of the seventeenth century, inherited a relatively rich literary tradition even in the silver-mad Villa Imperial de Potosí.

Of all the episodes in Potosí's history, the civil wars between the Basques and the "Vicuñas" (so-called from the fur on the hats they wore, as distinctive as Texas hats and boots today) were the best documented.[20] War attracts historians, and the civil wars that desolated the mining center between 1622 and 1625 were no exception. Arzáns stated that he had available eight printed works as well as five manuscript histories from which he extracted "the most convenient and the least scandalous data." Besides these formal histories, Arzáns quoted verbatim from a number of letters and other sources, especially the statements of various leaders of the opposing bands explaining and justifying their actions. The historian has given his readers the impression that as he wrote he sat surrounded by all kinds of evidence on these calamitous years in the Villa Imperial.

The cruelties these rival bands inflicted on each other exceeded those of Rome, France, and Granada, we are assured, for it was war to the death. The events were related in tremendous detail, often the exact hour being given of a particular encounter, and at the height of the conflict in February, 1624, a day-by-day record was provided. At the end of each year a statistical report on the damage was rendered. We are told how many were killed, how many wounded, the number of robberies committed, and the number of houses destroyed.

The flow of blood stopped from time to time because Potosinos could not live without fiestas. In 1622 they interrupted their preparations for war long enough to commemorate properly the death of Philip III, and on June 20, 1624, they began weeks of costly celebrations to honor the canonization of St. Ignatius of Loyola. No expense was spared; Arzáns recounted with delight the grandeur of it all, based on an account he said was printed in Seville. For fourteen days there were masses and sermons with impressive quantities of white wax burned, after which the streets of Potosí were gloriously decorated; and on every hand one saw remarkable tableaux, which Arzáns described in loving detail. The pious Potosinos marched up and down in procession along their richly decorated streets for a couple of weeks, rested up for a couple of days, then went on for another fourteen days of public rejoicing, which included bullfights, jousts, tournaments, and various theatrical spectacles. Whether all this expense of pesos and energy was really possible for a community that had waged fratricidal war for two years remains to be seen after more archival investigation, and it may turn out that Arzáns magnified this interlude of gaiety and peace as a literary device to give his readers some relief from the terrible story he had been telling.

The truce ended, a priest was killed as well as a child, and the war resumed. But the end of the bloody conflict was in sight. At last the fighting ceased in 1625 after prolonged and intricate diplomatic negotiations; peace was agreed upon in the Franciscan church by the contending parties and was sealed, as in the case of European wars, by the marriage of the daughter of one of the leaders to the son of the captain of the rival band.

The only aspect of the civil wars which Arzáns analyzed as a historian was that problem posed by every war—who or what caused it? He rejected the accusation that the Basques were chiefly at fault and held that both sides committed equal blunders. He believed that the sins of the Potosinos and the influence of the stars were together responsible but also quoted Captain Méndez approvingly, who had pointed out that men who arrived at Potosí as humble and peaceful citizens were soon transformed into demons by the effect of the silver there. Historians today may see economic, political, familial, and provincial reasons for the bitter and bloody conflict. But always there was present the widespread and overwhelming desire for wealth, desire increased to explosive proportions by the feverish atmosphere of the Villa Imperial. One historian Arzáns quoted, the Jesuit Alonso de Ovalle, was convinced that the Mountain of silver itself had a magical effect on the Potosinos and turned all those who lived in its shadow into fearless, restless, and revolutionary men.[21]

Ovalle's explanation for the ills of Potosí may be quite sound. From its earliest days the City had attracted the most daring, unscrupulous, and silver-thirsty foreigners as well as Spaniards.[22] Though José de Acosta praised and wondered at the great security of the long and lonely silver route from Potosí to the Peruvian coast, the Villa Imperial lived a rough-and-tumble life from its beginning. A spectacular robbery occurred in 1561, and a report of 1564 mentioned the "prejudicial presence of many foreigners—Greeks, Italians, Corsicans, French, Germans, and Portuguese."[23] So many vagabonds were found in Potosí that the crown frequently ordered the royal authorities to induce them "with discretion and skill" to go off to war against the Indians or on dangerous exploring expeditions. The civil wars of 1622–1625 attracted bold men from far and wide, reported Arzáns, as each side called upon its friends and relatives in distant parts to rally round. The royal officer appointed to pacify the embattled City reported that he could not find six men in all the town in whom he had confidence. Arzáns gives us a dramatic picture of the social anarchy of these years when Spanish individualism joined with a thoroughly materialistic society to produce the most agitated period of all the stormy history of Potosí.

Arzáns evidently wished to be considered a historian devoted to the truth, but one who worked as an amateur. He did not attempt to exploit systematically the archives in either Potosí or in La

Plata; the manuscripts he referred to in the *History* apparently had come to his attention by chance, or at least without any great effort on his part. A formidable list could be compiled, however, of the royal orders, *relaciones, informes,* poetry, financial records, and other manuscript materials which he scattered so prodigally from the beginning to the end of his story. All that can be given here are representative samples of these materials.

The large number of unpublished histories and other manuscripts bearing on the civil wars has been mentioned. Royal orders constituted such an important part of the life of Potosí that Arzáns naturally included them, as well as viceregal provisions, and decisions of the audiencia. Religious history, miracles, the lives of saints, and indeed everything related to the church held special interest for Arzáns, and he even quoted the private letters of ecclesiastics. From the many references to his sources, one might almost believe that he had a kind of divining rod, and that everywhere he went useful documents turned up. He gave many data on the silver production officially recorded, but he also knew about the unregistered silver illegally shipped out through Buenos Aires without payment of the royal fifth. It so happened, he said, that one Pedro Muñoz de Camargo kept count of the illegal shipments, which amounted to the sum of 560 million pesos in 112 years—a calculation based on that observer's reports plus similar accounts from other ancient citizens who had a similar curiosity about clandestine silver shipments.[24]

No one knows how many of these manuscripts Arzáns so assiduously cited actually existed at the time he was writing or whether he depended heavily on oral tradition. In any case, clearly Arzáns wanted to give the impression that he was a historian who respected original sources and had a great arsenal of them as the basis for his *History*. Some of the books he so confidently referred to may never even have been in his hands. Dr. Mendoza believes that Arzáns cited certain authors secondhand, though for the first half century of the story the *History* seems to rest on many well-known printed works. Materials for the later periods are somewhat limited, and it is possible that the most significant help the printed works gave him was not so much the information they contained as their influence on his idea of what history was and how it should be written.

The most direct and pervasive influence Arzáns received from his printed sources seems to be from the Augustinian friar Antonio de la Calancha, the first important historian to be born in the nearby city of La Plata, to whose *Crónica moralizada* Arzáns frequently refers.[25] Not only was Calancha a native of La Plata, but he had served as a preacher in Potosí; and his luxuriant prose shows that he partook of the spirit of Potosí, which he called "unique in its opulence, first in its majesty." He believed in astrology—so did Arzáns—and wrote the now famous description of the Villa Imperial: "In Potosí the signs of Libra and Venus predominate, and thus most of those who live there incline to be covetous, friends of music and festivities, zealous in the pursuit of riches, and somewhat given to venery." The boastful spirit of Potosí had affected him also, for he calculated that his convent had been given 535,000 pesos by 1611 and enthusiastically claimed that the Augustinian chapel and house were the finest in Potosí. In one month Potosinos burn more wax in their churches than Europe consumes in a whole year, he exulted. Calancha had much of the American pride of a New World Spaniard and felt that Spaniards not only improved themselves materially after reaching the New World but also were "more clever and able" than they had been in Spain. The wealth of Potosí has much influenced events in the motherland, he insisted. More students now go to the universities in Spain, more books are printed there, and "more maidens are married today in one year than before in forty."[26]

Calancha's *Crónica moralizada* was full of moralizing digressions, and he never forgot that he was a preacher; his pages were full of religious processions and edifying tales of piety and penitances. If one accepts his version of history, Potosí rivaled the viceregal capital Lima itself, which "passed its days in a continuous fiesta . . . they spent all their time tolling the bells and shooting off rockets. Any event, no matter how minor, was a pretext for noisy and ostentatious ceremonies, processions, illuminations and bullfights."

Calancha also expressed pity for the poor Indians, oppressed by their cruel taskmasters, as did

Tarapaya, a famous lake to the west of the City, whose water provided energy for mills (ingenios) to grind the ore. The valley of Tarapaya was temperate; corn, potatoes, and vegetables were grown there, and warm springs made the region a favorite recreation center for the inhabitants of Potosí. Note the houses for warm baths in the upper right and the village of Tarapaya in the lower right. The stream which connects with the aqueduct (ribera) for the mills of Potosí is depicted running all the way across the lower part of the illustration. From the Brown University Library manuscript copy of Arzáns' History.

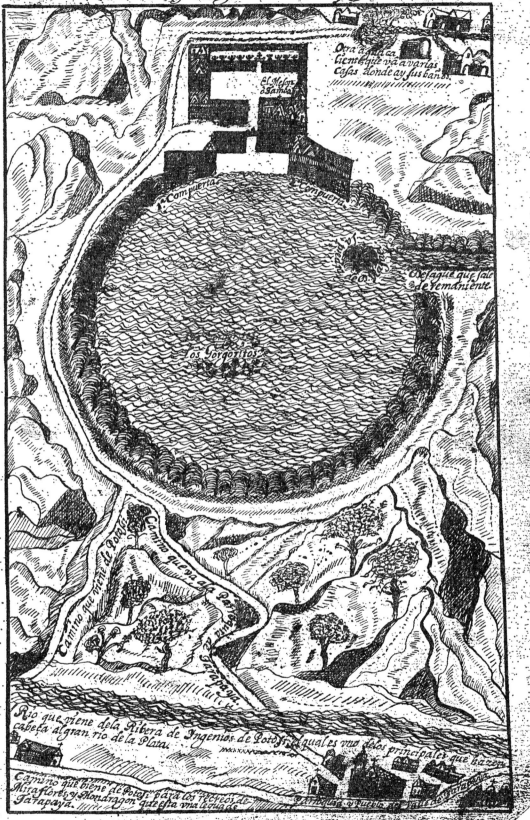

several other authors Arzáns quoted. Calancha attributed the great decreases in Indian population to their ill-treatment through the forced labor system called the *mita*. Arzáns included many of Calancha's anecdotes, accounts of monstrosities of nature, supernatural beings, and even the report that there existed in Peru a "university of witches, with professors giving instruction in the diabolical arts."[27] No breath of the brisk winds of the Enlightenment blows in either Arzáns' *History* or Calancha's *Chronicle* which he so much quoted.

After about 1715 Arzáns relied more on his own personal observations than on printed or manuscript sources. The co-editor of the *History,* Dr. Mendoza, has noted that from that date onward Arzáns was in effect mostly describing the events of his own day like a newspaper reporter. He gave the impression that he walked about Potosí discussing affairs with all manner of men, feeling the public pulse on many events. Thus he probably reflected rather faithfully the views of the people on many of the events he included in that part of the *History* covering the years 1715-1736.

Arzáns set great store by personal observation, his own or that of such frequently quoted earlier writers as Captain Méndez or Antonio de Acosta.[28] He stressed his own efforts to give eyewitness reports: he measured the depth of nearby Lake Tarapaya where rich miners' families bathed, he himself swam in its dangerous waters and observed curious incidents there, he discussed European events of the day with foreign visitors to Potosí whom he cultivated, and he was acquainted with certain wealthy persons despite their lives steeped in sin. Although devout and even conspicuously pious, Arzáns evidently had the spirit of a journalist who does not hesitate to mix freely with all kinds and conditions of men and women as he gathered material for his history.

And yet the *History* was somewhat like a Greek drama, in that much of the action took place off stage, and messengers brought news of miracles, tragedies, and other events. Only rarely does the reader catch a glimpse of the mines themselves. Potosí, the opulent, pious, and licentious City, was the stage for Arzáns; the Mountain honeycombed with the mines that produced the wealth that supported the Imperial City was decidedly off stage.

But once Arzáns himself climbed the Mountain and went as a visitor down one of the great shafts. There he had a terrifying experience; for the lights of the party went out, they had to wait in the dark for many hours until a miner passed by and helped them, and only after a long delay did they regain the surface of the mine. This harrowing experience and his disgust when he once ventured to chew coca leaves—a traditional practice for Potosí miners then and today, too, since it acts as an anesthetic making their labor more tolerable—reveal our historian as a tenderfoot in mining operations and the rough mining life. He may have been present when some new mining machinery was inaugurated near the City, but he generally avoided the great Mountain full of its many dangerous shafts. The life of the Indian miners he described with horror. The cries of the Indians at work in the bowels of the Mountain, the brusque orders of the Spanish masters, the noise of the frequent explosions, the sight of Indians sweating and stumbling up and down the narrow ladders by which they carried out the ore—stories such as these and other eyewitness accounts of men and events scattered throughout the text of the *History* reveal his concern to assure readers that his work rested upon fresh, personal observations as well as upon historical documentation.

Arzáns constantly lamented that he could not use all the sources at his disposal for the full story of the Imperial City.[29] He simply could not tell as much as he knew. The punishment that fate meted out to Potosinos in 1719 would alone have filled a large volume. At times the details of an incident were simply too abominable to include, lest his readers might be distressed. He was worried by the growing pile of his manuscript pages and noted down how much each folio of paper cost. Though his text was eventually to become one of the largest histories ever written in an age when writers did not count words, he disclosed over and over again to the reader that he had to deliberately omit much that he would have liked to include. For Arzáns' self-discipline his twentieth-century editors and his readers can only be profoundly grateful.

Some known persons and events were left out entirely. He never referred to the greatest painter in Potosí, the seventeenth-century Melchor Pérez Holguín, or to the compendious treatise on

Indian labor by Nicolás Matías del Campo y de Larrinaga.[30] Even more strangely, he did not mention the scientific-minded priest, Álvaro Alonso Barba, who printed in 1640 one of the few significant works on metallurgy in colonial Spanish America.[31] Barba had acquired his knowledge of mining methods during a long residence in Potosí. His *Arte de los metales* was well known throughout the viceroyalty of Peru and even reached to Spain, for he was called to Spain to apply to the famous Río Tinto mines there the experience he had developed in Potosí. Thus the silence of the *History* on scientific contributions of a Potosino is all the more noticeable. The absence of the notorious Catalina de Erauso from the pages of the *History* is also a surprising omission, for this nun-lieutenant who dressed and fought like a man and who had spent part of her astonishing career in Potosí is nowhere mentioned by Arzáns. No one, however, who reads the entire *History* will ask for more exciting or fantastic stories to be added to the present narrative.

The human and manuscript sources Arzáns tapped were thus erratic. He never seemed to be in close touch with the town fathers, or to have gained access to the municipal archives. He had intimate contacts with ecclesiastics, however, and not only received information from them for the *History* but also allowed them to see the manuscript and had the satisfaction of hearing sermons based on it. This reinforces the conclusion that our historian was neither rich nor powerful, held no important position in government, and occupied a modest place in Potosí life. What satisfaction must this quiet man have enjoyed, then, hoping that it would be *his* history of the opulent and colorful society of the Imperial City that the world would eventually read.

III

ARZÁNS' WORK:
THE HISTORY DESCRIBED

ONE OF THE VIRTUES of the large history written by Bartolomé Arzáns de Orsúa y Vela is its rich detail on almost every aspect of the life of the silver City in colonial Peru. Its all-inclusiveness is almost overpowering and can only be described in general terms here; readers will have to dig out for themselves the complete story, just as men have dug for over four centuries to extract silver and, later, tin from the mines themselves.

Arzáns showed no special knowledge of technology, but his *History* contains a considerable amount of information on the kinds of minerals found at Potosí as well as on the methods developed over the years to exploit them. He knew as well as any mine owner the crucial importance of improving techniques, although he emphasized the great skill of the Indian miners and the methods they developed before the Spaniards arrived in 1545. For the first two decades, the ores ran so high in silver that primitive smelting furnaces sufficed. Then a severe crisis came. To emphasize how significantly the discovery of mercury in Peru by the Portuguese poet Enrique Garces and its application by Pedro Fernández de Velasco helped to solve the crisis, Arzáns gave much attention to the application of mercury in 1572 during the visit of Viceroy Francisco de Toledo to Potosí, which greatly increased the production of silver.[1]

Viceroy Toledo usually figures in history as a great lawgiver, the "Solon of Peru"; but he was also a determined urbanist who did much to better the conditions of life for all who had to endure the harsh climate of Potosí, by improving housing, widening streets, and by encouraging the building of churches. He also stimulated the construction of ore-grinding mills operated by hydraulic power.[2] Four rich miners offered, under prodding by the viceroy, to dig great lakes in hills above Potosí which would impound the summer rains. A *ribera,* or aqueduct, was prepared as well to conduct the water to Potosí and was officially opened in 1577 with a week-long fiesta. The growth of the City, both in production and in population, from all these improvements was impressive; the census Toledo took counted 120,000 inhabitants, according to Arzáns.[3] Thereafter the *History* returned time and again to the search for even better mining techniques. One problem, never fully resolved, was the flooding of mines. In 1721 a French engineer tried to drain off the enormous amount of water that had accumulated in the mine called Descubridora. The water was so deep that a royal man-of-war could easily navigate, Arzáns tells us with what must be a touch of Potosí exaggeration; at any rate, the French engineer who had contracted to do the job failed miserably after an expensive attempt and fled the City in debt.[4]

Mining accidents, the discovery of new veins, the innumerable devices and methods both Spaniards and foreigners worked out to extract every possible ounce of silver were all reported in the *History*. When the true dimensions of the technological contributions to mining in the Spanish American colonies are more carefully studied—the latest authority, Modesto Bargalló, believes that their advances were much more important than is generally recognized—the data imbedded in the *History* will provide a significant part of the story.[5]

Representation of an ingenio, *or mill, for smelting the ore. Surrounded by stout stone walls, each ingenio was an industrial complex where various kinds of furnaces and processes were employed to reduce the ore. Water impounded in the lakes above the City was conducted by a* ribera, *or aqueduct, to the ingenio where it provided energy for grinding the ore and for washing the metal. All phases of the work are depicted, from the time the ore arrived from the Mountain on the backs of llamas (upper right) until the silver in bars* (piñas) *was ready for transport to the seaport, hundreds of miles away, for despatch to Spain. Note the chapel (lower left) where Mass was celebrated. From the Brown University Library manuscript copy of Arzáns'* History.

Forma de los Ingenios en que se muelen los metales de plata en la Ribera de Potosi, el uno de dos cabeças, y el otro de una.

del Gremio, con otros treinta y dos señores Asogueros. Jugaronlas con mucha destreza, y gusto de toda aquella dilatada plaça, donde avia multitud de gente. Continuaronse las fiestas por otros ocho dias con varias invensiones, y regozijos, en que la Nobleza por su parte, los señores Asogueros por la suya, los dueños de minas, y Mineros por otra, y los Indios por su parte se señalaron todos en grandissimos gastos.

En el mes de Março deste dicho año, se acabaron, y pusieron en perfeccion cien cabeças de Ingenios, quedando otras doze començadas, que se acabaron despues, y con el tiempo se fabricaron otras veinte; y assi fueron por todas ciento y treinta y dos cabeças en espacio de quatro millas y media, como dizen Pasquier, y Dueñas. Y no se porque estas Autores cuentan por millas Italianas, y no por leguas Castellanas las distancias que se ofrecen referir en sus Historias. Y si como quieren que todo el espacio desta Ribera desde el primero hasta el ultimo Ingenio, tenga las dichas quatro millas y media Italianas, de las que comunmente tres hazen una legua española, y cada milla mil pasos, y cada paso cinco pies, y cada pie dos palmos de hombre, tendra segun esto, legua y media: aunque segun mi experiencia y parecer tendra cabalmente una legua y tres quartos della. Corre la fabrica desta Ribera por lo alto de las casas de Oriente, a Occidente, y viene el grueso arroyo por arcaduzes de piedra, y madera, que en muchas partes estan por el ayre sobre vigas muy altas, y parte la poblacion por dos quadras de la plaça

Even such a literary and imaginative historian as Arzáns thus had to pay attention to the distinctly technical details of machinery and techniques; he took time to be present a few months before his death at the first use made of a new invention to grind ore. All Potosinos had a profound interest in the amount of silver extracted from the Mountain; Arzáns could not help but treat the story of mining operations in some detail if he were to reflect accurately the concerns of his fellow Potosinos.

The Potosí that we see in the *History* was proud and opulent, pious and cruel, but not a center of learning.[6] Lima had its university and numerous colegios, and it was also the seat of an audiencia or royal tribunal, all institutions which attracted and developed men of learning. Books were published there, poetical discussions held, and the wits of the viceregal community were sharpened by frequent intellectual disputes. Nearby La Plata also enjoyed the presence of an audiencia, always a focus for cultural pursuits. Audiencias stimulated the writing of books and the composition of treatises, for these groups of contentious and learned royal officials found that one of the routes to advancement was the production of historical, legal, or political works. Two of the ablest advisors of the Viceroy Toledo were members of the La Plata audiencia in the sixteenth century, the Augustinian Calancha wrote his *Crónica moralizada* there in the seventeenth century, and La Plata became in the eighteenth century a center for political discussion at the University of San Francisco Javier.

But Potosí produced silver. Though Arzáns taught school, a fact we learn not from him but from his pupil Bernabé Ortega y Velasco, we find in the *History* little attention to books, music or education generally. Religious art he lavishly described. But none of the rich miners seems to have sent his sons back to Salamanca for the polish of a university education in Spain, and there is no mention of well-to-do young Potosinos attending the university in La Plata. Perhaps Potosí considered itself such a center of the universe that it was felt unseemly for any Potosino to go to another city for anything, particularly to La Plata, which tried to lord it over Potosí politically.

The theater constituted an exception, and the *History* has much information of interest to the literary historian. Arzáns described from 1555 onwards the dramatic representations which formed part of every religious commemoration or fiesta when Potosí celebrated some such event as the accession of Philip III to the throne or the victory at Lepanto over the Turks. Many plays were given, and some of them were staged by the Indians in their own language. A theater was built by 1616; one of the essential means for the entertainment and education of Potosinos was their attendance at religious and literary dramas. Indians, traveling theater companies, and even ecclesiastics participated in these productions. On the day of the glorious Saint Rose of Lima in 1721, for example, in addition to sermons, three religious plays were put on with much skill by some nuns, "to general rejoicing in Potosí." Though our knowledge of the theater in Potosí is much scantier than for Lima or Mexico City, the *History* demonstrates that the silver-happy miners enthusiastically supported the theater.

From other sources we know that books were shipped to Potosí from Spain, that poetry of some importance was written there, and that at least one poet of the early seventeenth century, Diego Mexía de Fernangil, found Potosí a safe and pleasant place for himself and his family.[7] One of the books he read during the cold nights was the Portuguese classic, *The Lusiads,* by Luis de Camoens; the copy he used is now a part of the remarkable collection of the Hispanic Society of America in New York City.

Probably the information Arzáns gives on the cultural life of Potosí is incomplete, and as the history of the Villa Imperial is further investigated a fuller picture will emerge. But it seems reasonable to conclude that cultural activities at Potosí were secondary to the principal passion of the silver center and that the desire of the Potosinos to exploit the rich veins of the Mountain dominated most of their lives, just as the great Mountain loomed above the City itself.

Arzáns manifested throughout the *History* an ardent devotion to everything connected with the church.[8] He enthusiastically loaded his narrative with so much detail in describing the churches, chapels, and convents, and the religious art in them, as well as religious events and personages, that his approach reminds one at times of a gushing society reporter today. He scattered miracles prodigally in his pages, and the devil was for him a familiar figure, who was usually exorcised by some saintly person. Masses were reported statistically in much the same boomtown spirit as silver production was recorded, and in general the reader is deluged with the minutiae of ecclesiastical life in Potosí. The virtues and experiences of many individuals were recounted at great length: of Friar Gaspar Martínez, who resisted grievous temptations; of Doña Mariana de Benavides, who saw remarkable visions; of Friar Gaspar de Villaroel, a most learned prelate; of Captain Francisco de Oyanume, who invited twelve poor persons to his dinner table every Sunday in "reverence for the twelve apostles"; of the Dominican Vicente Bernedo, described as a "precious mine of virtues," whose holy reputation inspired macabre attention after his death: devout Potosinos cut off his fingers and toes to preserve as relics.[9]

One notable characteristic of the *History* is the pious ejaculations Arzáns inserted with almost mathematical regularity on such topics as Avarice, Prayer, Love, Charity, Poverty, Ingratitude, Vanity, Death, Chastity, Destiny, and on the question of whether it is cowardly for men to weep. (The answer is No.)

Arzáns did not limit himself to exhortations, accounts of how silver production stopped short because of the sins of the Potosinos, portentous examples of repentance, hermits, processions to halt epidemics, homilies on how a rich man helped a poor man, fasts, sermons, mortifications, the miraculous sweating of certain statues, and strange figures that moved around mysteriously in cemeteries warning sinners or frightening evildoers. He also treated of more mundane matters such as ecclesiastical quarrels over whether a priest must enter a church bareheaded on certain occasions and other questions of protocol and precedence which sometimes disrupted the community and once resulted in the suspension of processions during Holy Week when the altercations became exceedingly hot. We also get some idea of how princes of the church acted and traveled. Arzáns gives an excellent description of the visit of Archbishop Diego Morcillo Rubio de Auñón to the Mountain itself as well as to the City. In short, the reader sees the religious life of this pious century in strong colors.

Perhaps the most lasting impression a twentieth-century reader receives from this eighteenth-century chronicle is the shocking contrast Arzáns brought out between the lot of the Indian miners sweating and dying in the dark recesses of the enormous Mountain and the baroque religious practices of the Potosinos in the City. Arzáns never attempted to portray the labor of the Indians in the mines as anything but nasty, hard, and dangerous. Our historian was not on the side of the exploiters; when an archbishop's cousin took 40,000 pesos for a trip to Europe, Arzáns commented: "In truth, it was the blood, sweat, and tears of the poor Indians that was the larger part of what he carried with him."[10] Yet a few pages later he gave this account of the effect of the Augustinian preacher Francisco de Romero on the sin-ridden Potosinos: "Men, women, children, old folk, great personages, humble persons, poor, rich, noble, plebians" all fasted, covered themselves with sackcloth and ashes, and mortified their flesh with hair shirts. After eight days of preaching day and night Friar Romero ended his mission with an enormous procession in which everyone in the Imperial City participated, carrying hundreds of large candles of white wax and making "great penitences" as they proceeded through the twisting streets and impressive plazas of Potosí.[11] Thus did Arzáns faithfully report both the greed and religiosity of the Potosinos.

The reader will also discover, amidst all the miracles, fiestas, and moral stories, considerable data on what most Potosinos probably thought about every day, the production of silver and its meaning for them. And although Arzáns dismissed at times economic matters such as a rise in prices as being "of no importance," there is an easily discernible materialistic tone throughout much of the *History*. He naturally had many pages on silver production and exhibited throughout a keen interest in the economic importance of the mines to the Spanish crown.[12] Since the court of the powerful emperor Charles V in 1544 could not pay salaries on time, or even provide for some of its own most pressing household expenses, the news of the great discovery of silver the next year in Potosí must have been welcome indeed. So specific were Arzáns' figures on the royal revenue from the silver production each year that he seems to have had at his side the official records kept by the king's treasury representatives, which was doubtless precisely the impression he wished to give. The prosperity of Potosí and its decadence were faithfully mirrored in these production figures. If we are to believe the naturally prejudiced exclamations of Arzáns, the economic health of the whole viceroyalty of Peru, and even of Spain itself, depended upon the amount of silver extracted from the miles of tunnels and twisting shafts under the Mountain of silver. He revealed dramatically how the kings of Spain, the viceroys in Lima, the royal officials in Potosí, and of course the miners themselves were always watching that barometer of their fortunes, the production statistics. Whatever the excitements in the City, the mining of silver went inexorably forward.

Whether Arzáns' information was reliable on this matter can only be determined when some future investigator checks his figures against the voluminous and as yet mostly untouched records in the archives of Spain and America. Even then some doubts will probably remain. The seventeenth-century friar Buenaventura de Salinas believed it impossible to discover how much silver Potosí had yielded because in many years as much as a third was not officially recorded. The royal officials responsible for collecting the royal fifth—the *quinto*—were zealous in repressing such illegal smuggling out of silver. But the miners were highly skilled in evading the law, and in fact smuggling in all forms became a mature art in Potosí. Another uncertainty lies in the amount of silver produced by the *capchas,* those Indians who worked the mines on weekends for their own profit. Was it all officially registered, or did some of that too escape the royal tax? A certain parallel with our own day suggests itself here when one reads of our own Internal Revenue Service's efforts to close loopholes in our tax structure.

Perhaps one may apply to Potosí production figures John U. Nef's conclusion about Central European silver production statistics: "Aristotle remarks that an educated man will not expect greater precision in answering any question than the nature of the subject allows. Even today it is doubtful whether, without sacrificing accuracy, silver production in Europe from 1450 to 1518 can be put in the form of statistical tables . . . The educated man will not ask for precise figures. He will content himself with general statements, containing many qualifications . . ."[13]

Arzáns also paid much attention to the numbers of people the mines supported. By 1555 there were 4,000 persons from Spain, "all nobles"; only two years later he records 12,000 Spaniards but still only 4,000 "good and noble citizens." The census by Viceroy Toledo in 1572 registered 120,000 persons, but this probably inflated figure included Negroes, Indians, and mestizos as well as Spaniards. Another official census, taken in 1610 with "particular diligence and care," indicated that there were 160,000 inhabitants.[14] Thereafter the population declined, particularly after the three great "destructions" of Potosí. The civil wars of 1622–1625 were the first, the breaking of the Caricari dam and resultant flood of 1626 were the second, and the debasement of coinage in 1650 was the third. Each "destruction" weakened the silver City, and after 1650 the recuperative energy of Potosí seems to have waned. Thereafter silver production and the population fell together, until there were only perhaps 70,000 inhabitants at the time Arzáns began to write about 1705. By 1713 the number had increased by 20,000 because famine in outlying districts had driven folk to the City, a famine so severe that the Indians were forced to kill their dogs for food, despite the great love they had for them. When the epidemic of 1719 struck, there were only 60,000 Potosinos, and the deaths from this scourge further reduced the population. Research may scale down somewhat the population figures Arzáns gave, but undoubtedly the number of persons at Potosí was still large during most of the period covered by the *History* in comparison with all other cities in Spanish America.

Much of the clothing, food, and drink for Potosí's inhabitants—Spaniards, Indians, and Negroes alike—came from elsewhere, sometimes from thousands of miles away. Prices inevitably were high. In 1559 the total cost, including wax, for the funeral honors of Charles V, reached 120,000 pesos.

At that time the Potosinos did not feel the pinch, but later, when production fell off, they began to complain of the high cost of everything, and one treasurer barely escaped with his life in 1568 when he raised the sales tax from two to six per cent. The wealthier citizens were levied upon regularly to support the numerous and costly fiestas and the sumptuous churches; frequently the king asked for, and received, donations for help against the Araucanian Indians on the southern frontiers of Chile. There were also many poor Spaniards in Potosí. The contrast between the wealth of some and the poverty of others was so great that in 1592 the town council had to establish an inn where the destitute could obtain food and shelter. The frequent exhortations of Arzáns on behalf of charity and his extravagant tales of how certain rich miners spent their substance helping the poor must have been grounded in the grim reality of life for many Potosinos.

Yet the markets of the Imperial City were ordinarily filled with goods from many parts of the world, and Arzáns quoted Cieza de León on the variety and richness of the goods offered for sale there. We know from other sources that goods from all over Europe were transported to the Indies, ranging from church statuary, flutes, and sardines, to camel skins and shoe trees, but the items in Potosí markets were something special.[15] Arzáns proudly boasted that even in the depleted times in which he wrote goods to the annual value of 7,800,000 pesos were brought by an "infinite number of ships" from nearly all the countries of the world, drawn by the magnetic power of Potosí's treasure:

There were silks of all sorts and knitted goods from Granada; stockings and swords from Toledo; clothes from other parts of Spain; iron from Viscaya; rich linen and knitted goods from Portugal; textiles, embroideries of silk, gold, and silver, and felt hats from France; tapestries, mirrors, elaborate desks, embroideries, and laces from Flanders; cloth from Holland; swords and steel implements from Germany; paper from Genoa; silks from Calabria; stockings and textiles from Naples; satins from Florence; cloths, fine embroideries, and textiles of excellent quality from Tuscany; gold and silver braid and rich cloth from Milan; sacred paintings from Rome; hats and woolen textiles from England; crystal glass from Venice; white wax from Cyprus, Crete, and the African coast of the Mediterranean; grain, crystals, ivory and precious stones from India; diamonds from Ceylon, perfume from Arabia; rugs from Persia, Cairo, and Turkey; all kinds of spices from the Malay Peninsula and Goa; white porcelain and silk cloths from China; Negro slaves from the Cape Verde Islands and Angola; cochineal dyes, vanilla, cocoa, and precious woods from Spanish America and the West Indies; pearls from Panama; rich cloths from Quito, Riobamba, Cuzco, and other provinces of the Indies; and various raw materials from Tucumán, Cochabamba, and Santa Cruz.[16]

Food constantly preoccupied the Potosinos, and the land for hundreds of miles about was scoured to provide it in necessary quantities. Horses from Chile brought fantastic prices because they were so high-spirited, mules came from Córdoba on the route to Buenos Aires, Indian slaves from southern Chile, coca from Cuzco and beyond, and European goods especially from Portuguese channels. All moved to Potosí irresistibly pulled by the insatiable market the Mountain of silver had created.

The road between Potosí and Buenos Aires was the axis around which the entire political economy of the Río de la Plata revolved.[17] This trade, almost all illegal according to the restrictive Spanish laws, enabled such merchants of Buenos Aires as Juan de Vergara to build up large fortunes.[18] Vergara and his friends were able to buy up in 1617 practically all the municipal offices of Buenos Aires and in effect took it over, evidently with profits from contraband trade. Offices in the Córdoba municipality were also purchased with Potosí silver by Buenos Aires merchants. Thus Potosí not only attracted goods from many parts of the world; its power also reached out to affect other cities in distant parts of the empire.

Arzáns gave much detail on this contraband trade; his account of the flood of French goods during the years he was writing is especially important. He named the French ship captains, described his talks with Potosí merchants engaged in this traffic, and told of a French surgeon performing an autopsy in Potosí in 1710, which, if true, is a remarkable event in the scientific history of Peru.[19] Recent studies[20] show that there was in fact a good deal of French commercial activity on the west coast of South America in this period, and the History provides us with a close view of it through the eye of a Potosino.

Indians occupied a special place in Arzáns' account.[21] He never allowed his readers to forget that the glorious story of the Imperial City depended upon the labor of the Indians: "without Indians, the Indies could not exist." Early in the *History* he interrupted his account of the conquest of Mexico to deny indignantly that the Indians were "brutes incapable of reason," a falsehood, he said, spread by the enemies of Spain to diminish the importance of the astonishing victories Cortez and his soldiers had won over the hosts of Montezuma. The Indians were astounded by the color, dress, and weapons of the bearded Spaniards, but "mere ignorance does not presuppose incapacity," and he pointed out that the Araucanian and Paraguayan Indians fought courageously and successfully against the best Spanish soldiers, including those with battle experience in Flanders.

He early stated his fundamental position: although most Indians could not read or write, the reason was not their stupidity but that "they do not concern themselves with such matters." The Indians of Peru, he said, show "rare ability, clear understanding, and decided perseverance." They have been able to practice all the professions, artistic as well as mechanical, and Indian craftsmen can build an altarpiece, a doorway, a tower, and even an entire building without knowing either arithmetic or geometry, let alone reading and writing, all of which caused great astonishment among the Spaniards. So notable was their capacity that King Charles II issued an order permitting the sons of Indian chieftains, governors, and nobles to be ordained to the priesthood after university education and theological training. This attitude colored all of Arzáns' subsequent comments on the Indians. Here we see clearly that the struggle to insure justice for the Indians was a live issue long after the great champions of the sixteenth century had asserted Indian rationality.

Later Arzáns remarked that some Spaniards felt contempt for Indians and castigated the poet Diego Dávalos y Figueroa, whose *Southern Miscellany,* printed in Lima in 1602, denounced them roundly. Dávalos was replying to "a certain modern author," possibly the sixteenth-century Indian defender Bartolomé de Las Casas, who had claimed that Indians were fully human and capable of learning many things. Dávalos called this a "notable error" and denigrated Indian culture in a way familiar to all who have read the standard accusations; in fact his charges remind one of the depreciatory remarks on Indian culture published in Madrid by Don Ramón Menéndez Pidal in 1963.[22] In boldly praising the capacity of Indians and in defending them from the charge of being "brutes," Arzáns manifested an attitude not at all common among the Spaniards of his time. Even today in Andean countries many people believe the Indians to be "subhuman" and in their treatment of Indians conduct themselves accordingly.

Arzáns indignantly rejected this low conception of Indian capacity and attacked Dávalos directly while describing the construction of the new Franciscan church. He marveled at how little appreciation was accorded the humble Indian craftsmen who made this splendid building possible.[23] He marveled too at the skill of the Inca emperor Yupanqui the Good for his building of the great Temple of the Sun in Cuzco; he also praised the ancient temple on an island in Lake Titicaca, even asserting that Inca monarchs surpassed in opulence the Egyptians, Persians, and Greeks. The Inca empires lasted longer, too, he pointed out.

Arzáns condemned the opinion some Spaniards held that the impressive Inca monuments still standing in Peru were the work of the devil and scorned Dávalos for believing that these monuments were constructed by giants of the past, not Indians. He admitted that Indians had learned much from the Spaniards, but this proved to him their innate ability. He recorded the names of the Indian artists whose work enriched the Franciscan church and lauded especially Sebastián de la Cruz who died while on the job and who, though illiterate, "was a remarkable craftsman in stone," who had also created the great tower of the Jesuit church, judged then and later as one of the architectural glories of Peru.

Like many Spaniards, Arzáns was deeply interested in Indian history and devoted much space to it. He indicated, too, how intimately Indians came to share the life and ceremonies of Spaniards in Potosí. In 1559 they pleaded to be allowed to march first in the funeral procession of Emperor Charles V. Although this position was refused, as it was feared that they might introduce some ceremony of their own, they were allowed to take part. Such a precaution was necessary. A famous incident occurred some years later in Cuzco when the Indians participated enthusiastically in a procession in honor of St. Ignatius of Loyola; they seized the opportunity to revive one of their ancient Inca dances without the Spaniards being aware of it until it was done.[24]

Arzáns never spared his readers the Spanish atrocities toward the Indians. God struck down with disease certain Spaniards who seized two beautiful maidens for their evil purposes, and the reprimand Philip II was alleged to have given Viceroy Toledo for beheading the Inca Tupac Amaru was quoted with satisfaction. The loudest lament for the Indians Arzáns reserved for the mita, that system of forced labor which the seventeenth-century jurist Juan de Solórzano Pereira called "a subject no less profound than the mines themselves."[25] This system, by which one-seventh of the able-bodied men from all the villages in a great area around Potosí were regularly drafted to the mines, brought dreadful consequences for the Indians.[26] To be sure, hospitals were established for them, "protectors" were appointed for them year after year, but they went on dying from accidents and overwork. Potosí's name was so terrible to them that Indians chosen in the villages for the mita were sent off to the sound of funeral music, and those who escaped destruction in the bowels of the mines usually returned to their villages in miserable condition—minus an arm or a leg, or debilitated by disease.

Those few Indians who somehow evaded the mita became rich, and some were even able to use the Spanish legal machinery to protect their interests, but the numerous protests against the system by ecclesiastics and others indicate that it was indeed a heavy burden. Occasionally a viceroy such as the Count of Lemos tried to suppress it, but the feelings of many Potosinos may be gauged from Arzáns' story of the fate of Friar Francisco de la Cruz who was working against the mita. He died suddenly one morning, many believed from poison. Despite all the official concern of the crown and the blood-curdling reports of ecclesiastics, the system continued in force until the end of the colonial period.

Arzáns actually sheds little new light on the workings of the mita. But he conveys to his readers and shares with them the confusion of mind and irresoluteness of those Spaniards who wanted to protect the Indians but who also understood that silver could not be produced without their labor. In many passages we see the author's dilemma as he tried vainly to reconcile his respect for Indian cultural achievements and his conviction of their dignity as human beings with the harsh realities of the crown's and the miners' ever-pressing demand for the silver which was the very life of Potosí.

Despite the somber picture Arzáns gave of the mita and its horrors, he shared the pride of all Potosinos in their City, and he somehow makes his readers feel this too. The desire to tell of its glories was Arzáns' reason for undertaking his great enterprise, to prove that no other city in the world quite equalled Potosí. Many foreigners believed this as well. The Portuguese knew of the discovery of the great Mountain of silver almost immediately and for generations thereafter tried unsuccessfully to find one for themselves in western Brazil.[27] England's military expenditures in the seventeenth and eighteenth centuries greatly exceeded her resources, and her lack of an independent silver supply made her all the more interested in trade by which she obtained silver.[28] Thus foreigners and Spaniards alike exalted Potosí, and this in turn swelled the pride of Potosinos.

The wealth of Potosí became a byword in Europe.[29] "As rich as Potosí" was often heard in the streets of Seville; Cervantes has Don Quixote telling Sancho Panza, "If I were to reward you as you deserve . . . the mines of Potosí would not suffice"; and in sermons preached at Portuguese autos-da-fé the Catholic church was hailed as "an earthly Paradise filled with flowers . . . a Potosí of wealth." Even Captain John Smith of Pocahontas fame declared: "Let not the meanesse of the word fish distaste you, for it will afford as good . . . gold as the mines of Guiana or Potassie, with less hazard and charge, and more certainty and facility."

Other centers of power in America such as Mexico boasted of their own grandeur and importance to Europe. But Potosí was always unique to its citizens and to outsiders. One learns that a certain miner, Antonio López de Quiroga, spent more than a viceroy, or a grandee of Spain. Writing even as Potosí was in a visible decline and when it was difficult to mount the splendid fiestas of the old days, Arzáns detailed lovingly the great fortune of this rich, religious and attractive Galician.

Even when the *History* became a scandal sheet full of murders, sexual crimes, battles, and cruelties of many kinds, Arzáns preserved a tone of recording portentous events worthy of Potosí. Grandeur was present even in his tales of sin, as well as violence and pride. "Burning with rage" was the phrase he usually employed to characterize a Potosino reacting to some real or fancied insult; "monster of riches" was one of his standard descriptions of wealthy miners. Referring to a certain Pole, he remarked complacently: "There is no region in the world from which men do not come to Potosí." Into stories of bloody encounters, widespread corruption, and revolting deeds he dropped the comforting assurance that Potosí welcomes strangers, cares for its poor, recognizes bravery, and revenges those who are harmed.

Fiestas were special events in the *History*.[30] Celebrations were held in many parts of the empire, but Potosí processions were grander, her bullfights were bigger and better, everything was done more lavishly. The fiesta explains what one eighteenth-century ecclesiastic meant when he declared that the needless expenditure of money was "an old disease of this land." Arzáns gave minute details of the organization and execution of fiestas, telling which guild was responsible for what; he also made clear that some of the wealthier citizens assumed heavy responsibilities to insure the fiestas' magnificence. European travelers did not often reach Peru, but when they did, they also fell victim to "Potosí fever," for one Frenchman solemnly reported that the streets of the City were paved with silver bars during fiesta days. If one had to select one symbolic institution through which the ethos of this silver City could be best seen, that institution would probably be the fiesta, and the *History* documents its history admirably.

Spaniards who crossed the ocean to the New World conducted themselves like gentlemen the moment they landed, no matter how humble their positions had been in Spain, according to Arzáns. As early as 1548 the Spanish Parliament had learned that Spaniards in the Indies quickly lost the habit of work and consumed without producing. Spaniards in Potosí were the least given to labor and quickly acquired a bad reputation. One royal official in 1585 called Potosí "a den of thieves" and Potosinos "a Babylonian people." Potosinos definitely did not follow the advice of Columbus, who urged his men to abstain from women, to fast, and to pray before setting out on a mining expedition.

The violence of the Potosinos was as notable as their pride or their eagerness for wealth without labor.[31] Arzáns described vividly the violence lying just under the surface. "This memorable city, always the scene of dreadful tragedies," was one of his constant refrains. A typical chapter included information on "lack of rain, hunger, deaths, robberies, injustices, poverty, and dissensions." Arzáns reported annual statistics on the number of murders much as he noted silver production or masses celebrated. No one was respected: women and friars were murdered atrociously, women killed their jealous lovers or even their own daughters. Women are "the ruination of virtue," wrote Arzáns, and men should beware of them. Traitors were beheaded and their heads placed on posts in the plaza. The governors sent out from Spain were worst of all; one hung ninety-six men in three years and many others were just as cruel. At one time, twelve fierce men calling themselves "The Twelve Apostles" ran about the city robbing people indiscriminately and "violating maidens and married women alike." The violent tenor of Potosí life which Arzáns ascribed to the influence of silver and the stars is so much like the fifteenth-century Europe the Dutch historian Johan Huizinga describes in *The Waning of the Middle Ages* that one sees why a nineteenth-century author used Arzáns' *History* to write a volume entitled *Chronicles of Potosí: Customs of the Medieval Age of Hispanic America*.[32]

Potosí was in fact a kind of microcosm of Spanish New World society, and Arzáns' opinions on its people are revealing. Toward the Indians he was most favorable; Negroes he usually showed as being cruel to the Indians or instruments of other men's hatreds. To Spaniards he devoted much attention, displaying a marked antipeninsular Americanist spirit. He was a strong partisan of those who, like himself, were born in the New World and waxed indignant against a viceroy who remarked that the only fault of a certain illustrious citizen of Potosí was that he was a Creole. The *History*, curiously, paid little attention to mestizos, although many Potosinos were of mixed Spanish and Indian blood. They fought, killed, became wealthy, sank into poverty and sin, exhibited religious zeal, and committed crimes like others. But they refused to be imposed upon; in one of his relatively few references to them Arzáns recounted how President Nestares Marín refused to put into effect a royal order requiring mestizos to pay a tax like Indians, explaining it would rouse so much resistance that Peru would be ruined.

Despite his strong sense of being a Creole and not a peninsular Spaniard, Arzáns was spectacularly and steadfastly loyal to the crown. He recorded no personal travel away from Potosí, not even to Lima, let alone Spain. Yet a strong sense of responsibility toward the crown and the empire pervaded all his work, which gave such royal events as births, marriages, coronations, and deaths the same prime treatment that we observe in the British Commonwealth today. No courtier in Madrid could have been more obsequious or more eager than our historian to set down details of Potosí's celebration of royal events and empire affairs; the victory over the Turks at Lepanto caused wild rejoicing in Potosí. Arzáns lived far from most other great centers of the empire, but the *History* brought news of earthquakes in Lima, affairs in Paraguay, troubles in Tucumán, depredations of Francis Drake, the naval battle against the French off Cartagena, battles in 1710 at Brihuega and Villaviciosa, and struggles against the Dutch on the high seas.

In devoting so much ink and paper to the crown and its glamorous activities, Arzáns may have been prudent rather than loyal. Or he may have been moved principally by his keen interest in dramatic events, for in many respects he was fundamentally critical of the mother country. It is possible, however, for the same person to feel loyalty to an institution and yet also feel free to describe in detail its shortcomings. The soul of the Creole must have been complicated and troubled by contradictory feelings.

The affairs of empire were expensive; Arzáns admitted the grave problem of devoting enough men and money to push back the warlike Araucanians in Chile who continually menaced Peru's stability. To expel the Scots in 1703 from Darien near Panama the viceroy ordered even ecclesiastics to contribute, a step which led to very bitter feelings against the archbishop who had the thankless task of collecting the tax from his own clergy. But it was paid, although one poor priest had to sell one of his two shirts to provide his share.

Thus Arzáns had a sense of empire although he saw history from the viewpoint of Potosí, not from the vantage point of viceregal Lima or the Council of the Indies in Madrid. The Imperial City was the center of his universe. He was a Creole, loyal to his king and the empire, but definitely a citizen of the New World. The *History* will be an important source for the study of how Spanish Americans began to be separated in spirit from the mother country until the revolutions of the early nineteenth century brought their full independence.

Another value of the *History* is the way it reflected faithfully the picaresque spirit of adventure of the period it recorded. Picaresque novels found a ready sale among Spaniards in America. One list of books known to have been sold in Potosí included, besides the ever-present religious tracts, manuals on the training of barbers and scribes, dictionaries, a legal treatise, a "curious work on the harm caused by the consumption of tobacco," and twenty-four copies of one of the most popular picaresque novels by Mateo Alemán.[33]

Such novels, read and reread in Potosí, could well have influenced Arzáns' style and approach. An outstanding Bolivian historian, the late Humberto Vázquez-Machicado, has analyzed the picaresque spirit as it developed in different ways in Potosí and in Spain. He wrote that whereas in Spain hunger and poverty created the literary type of the adventurer, in Potosí almost everybody was rich. The adventurer who reached Potosí without a penny became overnight a wealthy gentleman. He believed that Potosí and its fabulous history have significance precisely because of this picaresque spirit: "In comparing the vast differences between the ancient cities in Spain and the opulence of Potosí, one may see the Hispanic soul in all its greatness and all its poverty; its overweening pride, its greed, its cruelty, its spirit of vengeance . . . but also its nobility, its grandeur."[34]

The influence of Potosí in changing, or at least modifying, Spanish values will probably be recognized more and more as the work of Arzáns becomes better known.[35] Emphasis on honor rather than on wealth is deeply imbedded in Spanish history. In 1434 the Bishop of Burgos, a convert named Don Alonso de Cartagena, was given the task of persuading the Council of Basel to assign Castile precedence over England and declared: "Spaniards are not wont to prize great wealth, but rather virtue; nor do they measure a man's honor by the store of money but rather by the quality of his beautiful deeds, wherefore riches are not to be argued in this matter; for if we should mete out precedences according to riches Cosimo de Medici, or some other rich merchant . . . would come before the duke."[36] It was in this spirit that sixteenth-century Tomás López Medel, audiencia judge in both Central America and New Granada, wrote in his still unpublished "Treatise of the Three Elements" that minerals were of value "not for the greed and disorder of men, but in order that they may realize the excellence of their Creator and give thanks to him."[37]

Another characteristic trait of Spaniards has been their faithfulness to tradition, their resistance to change. As Sebastián de Covarrubias said in 1611: "Innovation is usually dangerous because it brings with it change from ancient usage."[38]

Yet even high-born Spaniards competed frenetically for silver at Potosí as owners of mines, as storekeepers, or as owners of taverns. A tremendous social mobility was the result, and the *History* is full of stories of fortunes won or lost overnight. Spaniards in many parts of the Indies thirsted after the wealth of Potosí, though they may never have reached the Imperial City. Perhaps in this lies one of the justifications for assigning the Imperial City a long and significant chapter in the history of Spain in America. Just as the vociferous and learned Dominican Bartolomé de Las Casas, although not the only defender of the Indians, most persistently captured the imagination of his contemporaries and later generations as the Defender, so Potosí exemplified, in the gaudiest and most memorable colors, the passion for wealth that drew many Spaniards to the New World. Arzáns gave a remarkably detailed view of the battle that went on in Potosí between this passion and those other Spanish traits: piety, honor, and a belief in the supreme importance of nonmaterial values.

The *History* provides information in abundance on that obscurely known period when the Spanish colonies in America were slowly growing in character and independence. The first two centuries of Spanish rule, approximately the years Arzáns treated, were a kind of crucible of Spanish America. Potosí's needs drew Indians from many parts of Peru, in a forced migration that had never before been seen in the land, for under Inca rule only Indians on royal business moved along the famous Inca highways. Negroes were brought to Potosí despite its altitude and rarefied atmosphere. Spaniards from all over Spain and all walks of life took part in the silver rush, and we are not surprised to learn from Arzáns that one of the miners was a descendant of Columbus. Foreigners and vagabonds crowded in also; a sort of wild west atmosphere pervaded the City. Potosí was even more a melting pot than other parts of the empire, for few white women could endure the climate and a large number of mestizos naturally resulted.

The Liberator Simón Bolívar paid tribute to the reputation for great wealth and grandeur which clung to Potosí even in its decline when he visited it in 1825 at the end of the wars for independence from Spain.[39] The City had shrunk to a shadow of its former self, but, mindful of its traditions, it prepared a flamboyant welcome of the sort Bolívar relished. Thousands of Indians were assembled in their colorful costumes to greet him on the outskirts of the City, and he moved toward Potosí under a series of triumphal arches about which gaily beplumed Indians performed a sort of ballet. As he approached the center of the City, two children dressed as angels were let down from the grandest arch of all and pronounced short speeches. Bolívar was bombarded with oratory during his seven-week stay, but he was equal to it and repaid in kind. In one day he gave "elegant and appropriate *ex tempore* replies" on seventeen different occasions, and his days and nights were full of bullfights, formal dinners, balls, fireworks, and "other signs of public rejoicing."

Captain Joseph Andrews, who arrived in Potosí on October 15, 1825, "on behalf of the Chilean and Peruvian Mining Association," was immediately invited to a ball by that picturesque British general William Miller, a veteran of the revolutionary wars who was then serving as prefect of the Imperial City. Captain Andrews found at the ball "the illustrious Bolívar, the brave Sucre, the politic Alvear, the gallant Miller, Generals Santa Cruz and Urdinines, in short, all the heroes of the Andes. A galaxy of military splendour and dazzling uniforms, which seemed to excite the highest admiration among, and to awaken all the attractions of the ladies of Potosí."[40] Andrews found the Mountain an impressive sight: "If the mind of the observer can separate the sum of moral evil it has inflicted on the world from the bare view; no sterile object in nature can be more truly magnificent . . . the numerous metalliferous tints with which the cone is patched and coloured, green, orange, yellow, gray, and rose colour, according to the hues of the ores which have been scattered from the mouths of the mines, are singular and beautiful in effect."[41]

It was a period of gay receptions, a three-day fiesta, and other rejoicings, for the wars had ended and General Miller had thoughtfully laid in a supply of champagne, then a new beverage to Potosinos, as well as other luxuries. On October 25 Bolívar ascended the Mountain itself, accompanied by General José Antonio Sucre "and all the persons of distinction in Potosí." The ascent was made at the end of the winter season while raw winds still whipped around the top of the Mountain, but the ceremony was carried out with pomp and, of course, oratory. General Miller reported that the ceremonies included "a sort of collation at the summit,"[42] accompanied by patriotic toasts, probably with the champagne. With the flags of newly liberated Argentina, Colombia, Chile, and Peru flying in the breeze, Bolívar declaimed:

> We come victorious from the Atlantic coast. In a fifteen year struggle of gigantic proportions, we have destroyed the edifice of the tyranny constructed . . . during three centuries of usurpation and violence. The miserable remnants of the lords of this world were subjected to the most degrading slavery. What a great pleasure it is for us to behold so many million men restored to their rights through our perseverance and our efforts. As for myself, standing here on the mountain of silver called Potosí, whose magnificently rich veins provided for three hundred years the treasury of Spain, I consider this opulence to be of no importance when compared with the glory of having borne the standard of liberty victoriously from the tropical shores of the Orinoco to plant it here on the peak of this mountain which is the admiration and envy of the world.[43]

The spirit of New World independence, which began to be felt not long after Columbus sailed westward into the Ocean Sea and which the *History* we have been reviewing records so strikingly, reached a very Spanish kind of climax with the words that Bolívar shouted into the wind on the silver Mountain of Potosí. For the Liberator, at the very moment when he celebrated the final act of political independence from the mother country, was also proclaiming one of the fundamental ideas deeply imbedded in Spanish character—that men ought to seek virtue, not wealth. Who could more dramatically illustrate the power of Spain to mold her people than the successful revolutionary General Bolívar, standing among his brilliantly uniformed officers at the summit of the desolate Mountain high in the Andes that had been for centuries one of the principal producers of wealth in all the territory once ruled by Spain?

APPENDIX

AN ENGLISH TRANSLATION OF THE
CHAPTER HEADINGS OF THE *HISTORIA DE LA VILLA IMPERIAL DE POTOSÍ*

[*The page numbers refer to the Brown University Bicentennial Edition.*]

VOLUME II

BOOK VIII

BOOK III

NOTES

NOTES

INTRODUCTION

1. José de Acosta, *Historia natural y moral de las Indias* (Seville, 1590), Libro IX, capítulo ix.

2. Pedro de Angelis, *Colección de obras y documentos relativos a la historia antigua y moderna de las provincias del Río de la Plata* (Buenos Aires, 1836), II, 1.

3. Gustavo Adolfo Otero published the first fifty chapters with an introduction in the following way: Nicolás de Martínez Arzanz y Vela, *Historia de la Villa Imperial de Potosí (MDXLV–MDLXXVII). Riquezas incomparables de su famoso cerro. Grandezas de su magnánima población. Sus guerras civiles y casos memorables* (Emecé Editores: Buenos Aires, 1943). This volume and the reprint of it in 1945 were brought out under the auspices of the Fundación Universitaria Patiño of La Paz, Bolivia.

The chapters included in the Otero volume correspond to the material in the Brown University Bicentennial Edition, Bartolomé Arzáns de Orsúa y Vela, *Historia de la Villa Imperial de Potosí*, Lewis Hanke and Gunnar Mendoza, eds. (Providence, 1965), I, 1–166 (less than a sixth of the total manuscript). The text used for the volume printed in Buenos Aires was the manuscript copy of the *History* in the Biblioteca Nacional (Sucre, Bolivia). The Sucre MS is shorter than the Brown and Madrid MSS and apparently was copied by a scribe in a hurry.

4. See Arzáns, *Historia*, III, 470–478, for a more detailed statement on Colonel Church. An English version of this statement, "A Note on the Life and Publications of Colonel George Earl Church," will appear in Volume XX of *Books at Brown* (Friends of the Library of Brown University: Providence, 1965).

5. Dr. Mendoza provides an expert and detailed "Análisis de los manuscritos de la historia de Potosí utilizados para esta edición," Arzáns, *Historia*, III, 461–469. His conclusion is that both manuscripts are copies, that the Madrid manuscript was begun in 1710 and the Brown manuscript after that date, and that the Brown manuscript probably is a revised and enlarged copy of what he terms the "texto primitivo" of the original manuscript. There was an evident intention by the copyist to improve the Brown manuscript by making its text "más claro, más intenso, más completo y más rico" (p. 467).

6. The introduction by the editors, "Bartolomé Arzáns de Orsúa y Vela: His Life and His Work," runs to 181 double-columned pages, the text of the *History* requires 1,343 double-columned pages, and the following specialized studies are included in the Appendices in Volume III: José de Mesa and Teresa Gisbert, "Information on Art in the Work of Bartolomé Arzáns de Orsúa y Vela" (pp. 439–460); Gunnar Mendoza, "Analysis of the Manuscripts of the History of Potosí used in this Edition" (pp. 461–469); Lewis Hanke, "A Note on the Life and Publications of Colonel George Earl Church" (pp. 470–478); Gunnar Mendoza, "Preliminary List of the Governors of Potosí, 1545–1738" (pp. 479–485); Guillermo Lohmann Villena, "The Viceroys of Peru, 1544–1745" (pp. 486–487); Lewis Hanke, "Silver Production in Potosí" (pp. 488–491); and Gunnar Mendoza, "Unpublished Sources for the History of Potosí" (pp. 492–500). All the material in this edition is in Spanish.

7. Arzáns, *Historia*, I, xc–cxxvii.

8. For a complete list, see *ibid.*, III, 501–502.

CHAPTER I

1. Bernal Díaz del Castillo, *Historia verdadera de la conquista de la Nueva España*, Ramón Iglesia, ed. (Mexico, 1943), I, 259.

Part of the material in this chapter is based upon previous writings by the author: *Bartolomé de Las Casas, Bookman, Scholar, and Propagandist* (Philadelphia, 1952); "The Other Treasure from the Indies during the Epoch of Emperor Charles V," *Karl V. Der Kaiser und seine Zeit*, Peter Rassow and Fritz Schalk, eds. (Cologne, 1960), pp. 94–103; "The Dawn of Conscience in America: Spanish Experiments and Experiences with Indians in the New World," *Proceedings of the American Philosophical Society*, CVII, No. 2 (1963), 83–92.

2. Marcel Bataillon, "Novo mundo e fim do mundo," *Revista de História*, No. 18 (São Paulo, 1954), p. 350.

3. Richard M. Morse, "Some Characteristics of Latin American Urban History," *American Historical Review*, LXVII (1962), 336.

4. See the author's *Aristotle and the American Indians* (London and Chicago, 1959), chap. viii.

5. Francisco Romero, *Sobre la filosofía en América* (Buenos Aires, 1952), p. 125.

6. Roger B. Merriman, *The Rise of the Spanish Empire in the Old World and the New* (New York, 1918–1934), III, 45.

7. As quoted by Pál Kelemen, *Medieval American Art* (New York, 1943), I, 3.

8. Ramón Carande has some interesting remarks on this subject, *Carlos V y sus banqueros* (Madrid, 1943–1964), I, 357–358. As an illustration of the wealth of historical material on Peru alone, see Raúl Porras Barrenechea, *Las relaciones primitivas de la conquista del Perú* (Lima, 1937); *Fuentes históricas peruanas* (Lima, 1955); *Los cronistas del Perú, 1528–1650* (Lima, 1962).

9. As quoted by Daymond Turner, "Gonzalo Fernández de Oviedo's Historia General y Natural—First American Encyclopedia," *Journal of Inter-American Relations,* VI (1964), 267.

10. *Ibid.,* p. 274.

11. Harriet de Onís (ed.), *The Golden Land* (New York, 1948), pp. 7–8.

12. Howard F. Cline, "The *Relaciones Geográficas* of the Spanish Indies, 1577–1586," *Hispanic American Historical Review,* XLIV (1964), 341.

13. Arthur J. O. Anderson and Charles E. Dibble, *Florentine Codex: General History of the Things of New Spain* (Salt Lake City, 1950–1963), Books I–XII; Luis Nicolau d'Olwer, *Fray Bernardino de Sahagún, 1499–1590* (Mexico, 1952); Charles E. Dibble, "Pictorial and written sources for Middle American native history: Spanish influence on the Náhuatl text of Sahagún's *Historia," Proceedings of the XXXIV International Congress of Americanists* (1962), pp. 244–247.

14. See the suggestions for such comparative studies in *The John Carter Brown Library Conference: A Report of the Meeting Held in the Library at Brown University on the Early History of the Americas* (Providence, 1961).

15. Venancio de Carro, *La teología y los teólogos juristas españoles ante la conquista de América* (2nd ed.; Salamanca, 1951); "La 'Communitas Orbis' y las rutas del derecho internacional según Francisco de Vitoria," *Estudios filosóficas* (Santander, 1962).

16. Luis Capoche, *Relación general de la Villa Imperial de Potosí,* Lewis Hanke, ed. ("Biblioteca de Autores Españoles (continuación)," CXXII, 1–241 [Madrid, 1959]), pp. 41–68.

17. Antonio de León Pinelo, *Paraíso en el Nuevo Mundo,* Raúl Porras Barrenechea, ed. (Lima, 1943), II, 323–338.

18. Jorge Basadre, *La promesa de la vida peruana* (Lima, n.d.), p. 55.

19. Aurelio Miró Quesada Sosa, "Francisco Fernández de Córdoba, criollo del Perú," *Revista peruana de cultura,* I (Lima, 1963), 18–28.

20. *Ibid.,* p. 25.

21. Arzáns, *Historia,* I, 3.

22. *Ibid.,* I, Prólogo, 3, 22, 134, 176, 205; II, 22, 73, 156, 249, 321, 392, 440; III, 196.

23. See the Appendix (p. 45) for the English translation of the chapter headings.

CHAPTER II

1. Álvaro Jara has already produced a preliminary graph in his "Economía minera y historia económica hispano-americana: Notas sobre un programa de trabajo" (Mimeographed paper, Berkeley, 1965). An Italian version will appear in *Revista storica Italiana,* No. 1 (1965). See also the author's "Producción de plata en Potosí," Arzáns, *Historia,* III, 488–491; Lamberto de Sierra, "Razón certificada que se envió a Carlos III de las sumas que por razón de los reales derechos de quintos y diezmos han contribuido los caudales sacados del famoso Cerro de Potosí, desde el año de 1556 . . . hasta 31 de diciembre de 1783 . . ." *Colección de documentos inéditos para la historia de España,* V, 170–184.

2. Arzáns, *Historia,* II, 156.

3. Harold Wethey, "Mestizo Architecture in Bolivia," *Art Quarterly* (1951), p. 290.

4. This section is based on Arzáns, *Historia,* I, xxxiv–xxxviii.

5. *Ibid.,* III, 400.

6. This section is based on Arzáns, *Historia,* I, xxxviii–xliii.

7. The background and development of this destructive epidemic may be found in Henry F. Dobyns, "An Outline of Andean Epidemic History to 1720," *Bulletin of the History of Medicine,* XXXVII (1963), 493–515.

8. Arzáns, *Historia,* I, xlviii.

9. *Ibid.,* pp. xliii–xlv.

10. *Ibid.,* pp. xlv–xlviii.

11. *Ibid.,* III, 113–118.

12. *Ibid.,* I, xlix–lxiv.

13. *Ibid.,* pp. l–li.

14. *Ibid.,* pp. lii–liv.

15. *Ibid.,* p. 407.

16. See the author's "Um mistério bibliográfico: A 'História de Potosí' de Antonio de Acosta," *Revista portuguesa de história,* VII (1961), 5–10.

17. Arzáns, *Historia,* I, liv–lv.

18. *Ibid.,* II, 86.

19. Marcelino Menéndez y Pelayo, *Historia de la poesía hispano-americana* (Madrid, 1913), II, 273.

20. Arzáns, *Historia,* I, lvi–lix.

21. *Ibid.,* p. 323.

22. *Ibid.,* p. lviii; Inge Wolff, "Zur Geschichte der Auslander im Spanischen Amerika," *Europa und Übersee. Festschrift für Egmont Zechlin* (Hamburg, 1962), pp. 78–108.

23. "Carta del obispo de Charcas a su majestad, octubre 25, 1564" (Archivo de Indias), Charcas 135, No. 10.

24. Arzáns, *Historia,* I, 64.

25. *Ibid.,* pp. lx–lxii.

26. *Ibid.,* p. lxi.

27. *Ibid.,* p. lxii.

28. *Ibid.,* pp. lxii–lxiii.

29. *Ibid.,* pp. lxiii–lxiv.

30. Nicolás Matías del Campo y de Larrinaga, *Memorial apologético, histórico, jurídico y político . . .* (Madrid, 1671?).

31. On Barba, see Umberto Giulio Paoli, "Il metal-

lurgista spagnolo Alvaro Alonso Barba da Villa Lepe (1569–1662)," *Archivio di storia della scienza,* III (1922), 150–168; Henry F. Brieger, "Botanical Prospecting for Ore Deposits, used in Peru before 1600: Álvaro Alonso Barba," *El serrano,* XII (Lima, 1961), 7–9. For additional material, see the author's *The Imperial City of Potosí: An Unwritten Chapter in the History of Spanish America* (The Hague, 1946), p. 49.

CHAPTER III

1. I erroneously questioned Fernández de Velasco's priority in Capoche, *Relación general,* but Modesto Bargalló has recently established that Pedro Fernández de Velasco had experimented with the application of mercury as early as 1571 in Potosí and that Viceroy Toledo had ordered him to continue his operations there after Fernández de Velasco had demonstrated his method in Cuzco before the viceroy. For a detailed description of the manuscript evidence, see Professor Bargalló's valuable study, "Sobre la introducción en el reino del Perú del beneficio de amalgamación de las menas de plata de Medina," *Memorias del Primer Coloquio Mexicano de Historia de la Ciencia* (Mexico, 1964), pp. 143–167.

2. Much remains to be learned about the work of this administrator. It is to be hoped that the splendid manuscript in the Biblioteca Nacional (Lima) of the basic ordinances he promulgated will be printed someday with adequate notes and introductory material.

3. Arzáns, *Historia,* I, 158.

4. *Ibid.,* p. lxvi.

5. Bargalló, *Minería y metalurgia en América española* (Mexico, 1955), pp. 112–114, 351–352.

6. Arzáns, *Historia,* I, lxvi–lxvii.

7. José Toribio Medina, *Biblioteca hispano-americana, 1493–1810* (Santiago de Chile, 1898–1907), II, No. 538.

8. Arzáns, *Historia,* I, lxvii–lxix.

9. *Ibid.,* p. 314.

10. *Ibid.,* II, 466.

11. *Ibid.,* p. 473.

12. *Ibid.,* I, lxix–lxxiii.

13. John U. Nef, "Silver Production in Central Europe, 1450–1618," *Journal of Political Economy,* XLIX (1941), 591.

14. Arzáns, *Historia,* I, lxix–lxx.

15. José Torre Revello, "Merchandise brought to America by the Spaniards, 1534–1586," *Hispanic American Historical Review,* XXIII (1943), 773–781.

16. Arzáns, *Historia,* I, 8–9.

17. *Ibid.,* p. lxxi.

18. Raúl A. Molina, "Juan de Vergara, señor de vidas y haciendas en el Buenos Aires del siglo XVII," *Boletín de la Academia Nacional de la Historia,* XXIV–XXV (Buenos Aires, 1950–1951), 51–143. Miss Catherine Pares kindly called this article to my attention.

19. Arzáns, *Historia,* I, lxxii. The first autopsy in Chile for which documentation exists occurred in 1773.

See Enrique Laval, "Una autopsia en Chile en el siglo XVIII," *Historia,* II (Universidad Católica de Chile, Instituto de Historia, Santiago, 1963), 118–133.

20. Erick Wilhelm Dahlgren, *Les relations commerciales et maritimes entre la France et les côtes de l'océan Pacifique (commencement du XVIIIᵉ siècle)* (Paris, 1909); Sergio Villalobos R., "Contrabando francés en el pacífico, 1700–1724," *Revista de historia de América,* No. 51 (1961), pp. 49–80.

21. Arzáns, *Historia,* I, lxxiii–lxxvii.

22. Ramón Menéndez Pidal, *Bartolomé de Las Casas, su doble personalidad* (Madrid, 1963).

23. Arzáns, *Historia,* III, 16.

24. Philip Ainsworth Means, *Biblioteca Andina,* Part I ("Transactions of the Connecticut Academy of Arts and Sciences, Vol. XXIX [New Haven, 1928]), pp. 271–525.

25. Juan de Solórzano Pereira, *Política indiana* (Madrid, 1648), Libro II, capítulo xvi.

26. Arzáns, *Historia,* I, lxxvi–lxxvii.

27. Sérgio Buarque de Holanda, *Visão do paraíso: Os motivos edênicos no descobrimento e colonização do Brasil* (São Paulo, 1959), p. 117.

28. Curtis P. Nettels, "England and Spanish American Trade, 1680–1715," *Journal of Modern History,* III (1931).

29. The specific examples in this paragraph are to be found in Miguel de Cervantes Saavedra, *El ingenioso hidalgo don Quixote de la Mancha,* Francisco Rodríguez Marín, ed. (Madrid, 1922), VIII, 282; Edward Glaser, "Invitation to Intolerance: A Study of the Portuguese Sermons Preached at Autos-da-fé," *Hebrew Union College Annual,* XXVII (1956), 339–340; John Smith, *The General Historie of Virginia, New England, and the Summer Isles* (London, 1624), p. 219.

30. Arzáns, *Historia,* I, lxxix.

31. *Ibid.,* p. lxxx.

32. Vicente G. Quesada, *Crónicas potosinas: Costumbres de la edad medieval hispano-americana* (Paris, 1890).

33. Irving A. Leonard, "Pérez de Montalbán, Tomás Gutiérrez, and Two Book Lists," *Hispanic Review,* XII (1944), 275–287.

34. Humberto Vázquez-Machicado, "Resabios de la novela picaresca en el Potosí colonial," *Facetas del intelecto boliviano* (Oruro, 1958), pp. 338–339.

35. See the author's *Imperial City of Potosí: An Unwritten Chapter,* pp. 36–42.

36. As quoted by Donald E. Worcester, "Historical and Cultural Sources of Spanish Resistance to Change," *Journal of Inter-American Studies,* VI (1964), 177.

37. Tomás López Medel, "Tratado de los tres elementos . . ." (MS, Muñoz Collection, Academia de la Historia, Madrid), XXVII, fol. 212ᵛ. Miss Constance Crowder was kind enough to supply this information.

38. Worcester, "Historical and Cultural Sources of Spanish Resistance to Change," p. 178.

39. John Miller, *Memoirs of General Miller in the Service of the Republic of Peru* (2nd ed.; London,

1829). Chapters xxix and xxx in Vol. II contain abundant detail on Bolívar's visit and on Potosí at that time. See also R. A. Humphreys, *Liberation in South America, 1806–1827: The Career of James Paroissien* (London, 1952), pp. 149–152; Robert W. Delaney, "General Miller and the Confederación Perú-Boliviana," *The Americas* (1962), pp. 213–242.

The amount of detailed information on the revolutionary period is impressive. See Charles W. Arnade, "Una bibliografía selecta de la guerra de la emancipación en el Alto Perú," *Boletín de la Sociedad Geográfica y de Historia de Potosí*, XL, No. 12 (1953),

159–169. Two manuscripts in England of value are H. Czettritz, "Descripción del Cerro de Potosí" (Paroissien Papers, Essex Record Office, Chelmsford, Essex); J. B. Pentland, "Report on Bolivia" (2 Dec. 1827, Foreign Office 61/12).

40. Joseph Andrews, *Journey from Buenos Ayres, through the Provinces of Cordova, Tucuman, and Salta, to Potosí* (London, 1827), II, 89.

41. *Ibid.,* II, 112–113.

42. Miller, *Memoirs,* II, 301.

43. Vicente Lecuna (ed.), *Proclamas y discursos del Libertador* (Caracas, 1939), p. 314.

BIBLIOGRAPHY

BIBLIOGRAPHY

Acosta, José de. *Historia natural y moral de las Indias.* Seville, 1590.

Anderson, Arthur J. O., and Dibble, Charles E. *Florentine Codex: General History of the Things of New Spain.* Books I–XII. Salt Lake City, 1950–1963.

Andrews, Joseph. *Journey from Buenos Ayres, through the Provinces of Cordova, Tucuman, and Salta, to Potosí.* 2 vols. London, 1827.

Angelis, Pedro de. *Colección de obras y documentos relativos a la historia antigua y moderna de las provincias del Río de la Plata.* 6 vols. Buenos Aires, 1836.

Arnade, Charles W. "Una bibliografía selecta de la guerra de la emancipación en el Alto Perú," *Boletín de la Sociedad Geográfica y de Historia de Potosí,* XL, No. 12 (1953), 159–169.

Arzáns de Orsúa y Vela, Bartolomé. *Historia de la Villa Imperial de Potosí,* eds. Lewis Hanke and Gunnar Mendoza. Brown University Bicentennial Edition, 3 vols. Providence, 1965.

Bargalló, Modesto. *Minería y metalurgia en América española.* Mexico, 1955.

———. "Sobre la introducción en el reino del Perú del beneficio de amalgamación de las menas de plata de Medina," *Memorias del Primer Coloquio Mexicano de Historia de la Ciencia* (Mexico, 1964), pp. 143–167.

Basadre, Jorge. *La promesa de la vida peruana.* Lima, n.d.

Bataillon, Marcel. "Novo mundo e fim do mundo," *Revista de História,* No. 18 (São Paulo, 1954), pp. 343–351.

Brieger, Henry F. "Botanical Prospecting for Ore Deposits, used in Peru before 1600: Álvaro Alonso Barba," *El serrano,* XII (Lima, 1961), 7–9.

Campo y de Larrinaga, Nicolás Matías del. *Memorial apologético, histórico, jurídico y político . . .* Madrid [1671?].

Capoche, Luis. *Relación general de la Villa Imperial de Potosí,* ed. Lewis Hanke. ("Biblioteca de Autores Españoles (continuación)," Vol. CXXII.) Madrid, 1959, pp. 1–241.

Carande, Ramón. *Carlos V y sus banqueros.* 3 vols. Madrid, 1943–1964.

Carro, Venancio de. "La 'Communitas Orbis' y las rutas del derecho internacional según Francisco de Vitoria," *Estudios filosóficas* (Santander, 1962).

———. *La teología y los teólogos juristas españoles ante la conquista de América.* 2nd ed., 2 vols. Salamanca, 1951.

Cervantes Saavedra, Miguel de. *El ingenioso hidalgo don Quixote de La Mancha,* ed. Francisco Rodríguez Marín. 8 vols. Madrid, 1922.

Cline, Howard F. "The *Relaciones Geográficas* of the Spanish Indies, 1577–1586," *Hispanic American Historical Review,* XLIV (1964), 341–374.

Czettritz, H. "Descripción del Cerro de Potosi," MS, Paroissien Papers, Essex Record Office, Chelmsford, Essex.

Dahlgren, Erick Wilhelm. *Les relations commerciales et maritimes entre la France et les côtes de l'océan Pacifique (commencement du XVIIIᵉ siècle).* Paris, 1909.

Delaney, Robert W. "General Miller and the Confederación Peru-Boliviana," *The Americas* (Academy of American Franciscan History, 1962), pp. 213–242.

Díaz del Castillo, Bernal. *Historia verdadera de la conquista de la Nueva España,* ed. Ramón Iglesia. 2 vols. Mexico, 1943.

Dibble, Charles E. "Pictorial and written sources for Middle American native history: Spanish influence on the Náhuatl text of Sahagún's *Historia,*" *Proceedings of the XXXIV International Congress of Americanists* (1962), pp. 244–247.

Dobyns, Henry F. "An Outline of Andean Epidemic History to 1720," *Bulletin of the History of Medicine,* XXXVII (1963), 493–515.

d'Olwer, Luis Nicolau. *Fray Bernardino de Sahagún, 1499–1590.* Mexico, 1952.

Glaser, Edward. "Invitation to Intolerance: A Study of the Portuguese Sermons Preached at Autos-da-fé," *Hebrew Union College Annual,* XXVII (1956), 327–385.

Hanke, Lewis. *Aristotle and the American Indians.* London and Chicago, 1959.

———. *Bartolomé de Las Casas, Bookman, Scholar, and Propagandist.* Philadelphia, 1952.

———. "The Dawn of Conscience in America: Spanish Experiments and Experiences with Indians in the New World," *Proceedings of the American Philosophical Society,* CVII, No. 2 (1963), 83–92.

———. *The Imperial City of Potosí: An Unwritten Chapter in the History of Spanish America.* The Hague, 1956.

———. "Um mistério bibliográfico: A 'História de Potosí' de Antonio de Acosta," *Revista portuguesa de história,* VII (1961), 5–10.

———."The Other Treasure from the Indies during the Epoch of Emperor Charles V," *Karl V. Der Kaiser und seine Zeit,* ed. Peter Rassow and Fritz Schalk (Cologne, 1960), pp. 94–103.

———. "Producción de plata en Potosí," Arzáns, *Historia,* III, 488–491.

Holanda, Sérgio Buarque de. *Visão do paraíso: Os motivos edênicos no descobrimento e colonização do Brasil.* São Paulo, 1959.

Humphreys, R. A. *Liberation in South America, 1806–1827: The Career of James Paroissien.* London, 1952.

Jara, Álvaro. "Economía minera y historia económica hispano-americana: Notas sobre un programa de trabajo." Mimeographed paper, Berkeley, 1965.

John Carter Brown Library Conference: A Report of the Meeting Held in the Library at Brown University on the Early History of the Americas. Providence, 1961.

Kelemen, Pál. *Medieval American Art.* 2 vols. New York, 1943.

Laval, Enrique. "Una autopsia en Chile en el siglo XVIII," *Historia,* II (Universidad Católica de Chile, Instituto de Historia, Santiago, 1963), 118–133.

Lecuna, Vicente (ed.). *Proclamas y discursos del Libertador.* Caracas, 1939.

León Pinelo, Antonio de. *Paraíso en el Nuevo Mundo,* ed. Raúl Porras Barrenechea. 2 vols. Lima, 1943.

Leonard, Irving A. "Pérez de Montalbán, Tomás Gutiérrez, and Two Book Lists," *Hispanic Review,* XII (1944), 275–287.

López Medel, Tomás. "Tratado de los tres elementos . . ." MS, Muñoz Collection, Academia de la Historia, Madrid, fols. 125–263ᵛ.

Means, Philip Ainsworth. *Biblioteca Andina,* Part I. ("Transactions of the Connecticut Academy of Arts and Sciences," Vol. XXIX.) New Haven, 1928, pp. 271–525.

Medina, José Toribio. *Biblioteca hispano-americana, 1493–1810.* 7 vols. Santiago de Chile, 1898–1907.

Menéndez Pidal, Ramón. *Bartolomé de Las Casas, su doble personalidad.* Madrid, 1963.

Menéndez y Pelayo, Marcelino. *Historia de la poesía hispano-americana.* 2 vols. Madrid, 1913.

Merriman, Roger B. *The Rise of the Spanish Empire in the Old World and the New.* 4 vols. New York, 1918–1934.

Miller, John. *Memoirs of General Miller in the Service of the Republic of Peru.* 2nd ed., 2 vols. London, 1829.

Miró Quesada Sosa, Aurelio. "Francisco Fernández de Córdoba, criollo del Perú," *Revista peruana de cultura,* I (Lima, 1963), 18–28.

Molina, Raúl A. "Juan de Vergara, señor de vidas y haciendas en el Buenos Aires del siglo XVII," *Boletín de la Academia Nacional de la Historia,* XXIV–XXV (Buenos Aires, 1950–1951), 51–143.

Morse, Richard M. "Some Characteristics of Latin American Urban History," *American Historical Review,* LXVII (1962), 317–338.

Nef, John U. "Silver Production in Central Europe, 1450–1618," *Journal of Political Economy,* XLIX (1941), 575–591.

Nettels, Curtis P. "England and the Spanish American Trade, 1680–1715," *Journal of Modern History,* III (1931), 1–32.

Onís, Harriet de (ed.). *The Golden Land.* New York, 1948.

Paoli, Umberto Giulio. "Il metallurgista spagnolo Alvaro Alonso Barba da Villa Lepe (1569-1662)," *Archivio di storia della scienza,* III (1922), 150–168.

Pentland, J. B. "Report on Bolivia." (2 Dec. 1827). MS, Public Record Office, London, Foreign Office 61/12.

Porras Barrenechea, Raúl. *Fuentes históricas peruanas.* Lima, 1955.

———. *Los cronistas del Perú, 1528–1650.* Lima, 1962.

———. *Las relaciones primitivas de la conquista del Perú.* Lima, 1937.

Quesada, Vicente G. *Crónicas potosinas: Costumbres de la edad medieval hispano-americana.* 2 vols. Paris, 1890.

Romero, Francisco. *Sobre la filosofía en América.* Buenos Aires, 1952.

Sierra, Lamberto de. "Razón certificada que se envió a Carlos III de las sumas que por razón de los reales derechos de quinto y diezmos han contribuido los caudales sacados del famoso Cerro de Potosí, desde el año de 1556 . . . hasta 31 de diciembre de 1783 . . ." *Colección de documentos inéditos para la historia de España,* V, 170–184.

Smith, John. *The General Historie of Virginia, New England, and the Summer Isles.* London, 1624.

Solórzano Pereira, Juan de. *Política indiana.* Madrid, 1648.

Torre Revello, José. "Merchandise brought to America by the Spaniards, 1534–1586," *Hispanic American Historical Review,* XXIII (1943), 773–781.

Turner, Daymond. "Gonzalo Fernandez de Oviedo's Historia General y Natural—First American Encyclopedia," *Journal of Inter-American Relations,* VI (1964), 267–274.

Vázquez-Machicado, Humberto. "Resabios de la novela picaresca en el Potosí colonial," *Facetas del intelecto boliviano* (Oruro, Bolivia, 1958), pp. 338–339.

Villalobos R., Sergio, "Contrabando francés en el pacífico, 1700–1724," *Revista de historia de América,* No. 51 (1961), pp. 49–80.

Wethey, Harold. "Mestizo Architecture in Bolivia," *Art Quarterly* (1951), pp. 283–304.

Wolff, Inge. "Zur Geschichte der Auslander im Spanischen Amerika," *Europa und Übersee. Festschrift für Egmont Zechlin* (Hamburg, 1962), pp. 78–108.

Worcester, Donald E. "Historical and Cultural Sources of Spanish Resistance to Change," *Journal of Inter-American Studies,* VI (1964), 173–180.

INDEX

INDEX